30 Amazing things to do in

Puerto Rico

Pocket Guide to your Dream Vacation with activities from FREE to $20

Paperback ISBN-13: 979-8-9878590-0-1

Hardcover ISBN-13: 979-8-9878590-2-5

First edition

Please note that any pricing, availability, contact info and website addresses may change over time. Contact location directly to confirm details.

TABLE OF CONTENTS:

The Fundamentals

Introduction

This is not your typical travel guide packed with only sponsored "touristy" locations. We included only the cream of the crop "gem" locations for budget adventurers to pick from.

We believe everyone should experience all the pure beauty, history and culture that Puerto Rico has to offer regardless of budget. The focus of this book is to make it super easy for you to plan a magical vacation while spending as little as possible. Puerto Rico is composed of many islands and is truly a paradise on Earth and you need ZERO DOLLARS to enjoy the best parts of this wonderland.

We have compiled 30 of the best free & low cost alluring spots to enjoy no matter where you are on the island. For the purposes of this book we define free & low cost as priced from $0 USD to $20 USD per person. We have also included 3 amazing "Splurge Worthy" adventures for less than $100 per person for that extra special outing.

You will be able to search this guide by the type of activity you are looking for. We have broken them down by the following four categories; Water & Natural World Wonder Gems, Cultural & Historical Gems, Awe-Inspiring Social Media Photo Worthy Gem Spots and Splurge Worthy Gem Adventures.

These experiences range from relaxing to adventurous. We will not only save you money but time and frustration of having to search for the finest of all the affordable options for your trip.

Some spots are easy to find and are family friendly while others are harder to find and will require the right vehicle and/or physical strength/stamina/stability to enjoy. You will need a good GPS and/or maps to keep you on track. Keep in mind that some of the addresses may look different to you. The address may just be the road name with the KM road marker location that you will use to find the place. We know you will love every bit of Puerto Rico just as much as we did.

We also cover some key historical information, travel tips, island facts and essential authentic Puerto Rican foods to try. If you arrived via the San Juan Airport you are in luck as your first social media photo worthy shots are coming right up. There are huge alternating Puerto Rico & USA flags all along the entire bridge as you exit. To see the sheer size of them blowing in the wind was the perfect welcome to the island for us. If you are not staying in old San Juan we recommend bringing your walking shoes and spending at least one full day there to experience one of the most beautiful cities in the world. There are so many sites, streets, buildings and restaurants to encounter in this colonized city. Be sure to stroll down the bewitching Paseo de la Princesa promanage while there to see Fuente Raices, a breathtaking waterfront fountain and perfect place to watch the sunset on any day.

You can drive the entire island in about 4-6 hours; most of these ideas can be used as a day trip no matter where you are on the island.

So without further ado.

Asi Comienza

Let the adventures begin.

VERY BRIEF HISTORY OF PUERTO RICO

Puerto Rican history is Taíno History. Arriving from South America, the Taínos are the indigenous people of Puerto Rico and the Caribbean. The Taínos inhabited the land and called the island Boriken or Borinquen. This translated to "the great land of the valiant and noble Lord" or "land of the great lords". The Spanairds including Christopher Columbus arrived November 19, 1493 to the island on their second voyage to the "New World". These outsiders named the island after St. John the Baptist by calling it San Juan Bautista. When the foreigners first arrived; it is said that the Taínos did not resist the Spanish takeover as they believed they were gods.There is a Taíno legend that tells of a time where great gods would rise from the water. This made it easier for the Spanish to manipulate the population. The community would soon rebel and fight back. The Spanish began to use the people as slave laborers and even sent them back to Spain.

The island soon became a major trading and military outpost for Spain in the Caribbean. The Spanish named one of their first towns Puerto Rico, meaning "rich port" because of the gold and other materials found there. This community became so popular that eventually the entire island took on the name.

The Spaniards used violence and forced the Taínos labor in the silver and gold mines along with plantations. Over time, the natives began to resist the colonizers. In 1514, a rebellion resulted in about 80-90% of the Taíno population being slaughtered. It is thought that over 7 million Taíno died or were killed as a result of the Spanish Invasion. Since the Spanish eliminated their workforce they had to find a new workforce. The Spanish began to bring in African slaves to the island. It is said that the entire native population of Taínos were eliminated from the island by the early 1600's. The only survivors are said to be the children of Taínos that married either a Spainard or African slave. Today Puerto Rico has a rich diverse racial background and culture due to the mixes of Taíno, Spanish and African history.

Moving forward, at the end of the Spanish-American war, the Treaty of Paris was signed. On December 10, 1898; Spain relinquished all holds to Cuba. They also resigned their positions in regard to Puerto Rico and Guam to the USA. As well as their hold on the Philippines to the United States for $20,000,000.

The United States granted Puerto Ricans U.S. statutory citizenship on March 2, 1917. Today, there is much debate on Puerto Rico becoming the 51st state.

GEOGRAPHY FACTS

Location: Caribbean, island between the Caribbean Sea and the North Atlantic Ocean, east of the Dominican Republic.

Geographic coordinates: 18°15'N, 66°30'W

Region: North America

Subregion: Caribbean

Total Area: 9,104 sq km or 3,508 sq mi

Relative area: approximately three times the size of Rhode Island, USA

Borders: Puerto Rico is under the U.S. customs jurisdiction. Borders are open between P.R. and the U.S., allowing for free movement of persons and goods.

Coastline: 501 km

Elevation: *lowest point*: Caribbean Sea 0 m *highest point*: Cerro de Punta 1,338 m

Climate: The climate is Tropical Marine with average temperatures year round, near 80 °F (26.7 °C) in lower elevations and 70 °F (21.1 °C) in the mountains.

Hurricane season: June to November. Hurricane season represents an additional risk obviously however you save a lot of money in lodging and car rentals during this time. If possible protect your trip with travel insurance.

Rainy Season: April to November (carry a small umbrella with you)

Dry Season: December to May (most expensive time to travel)

Time Zone: Atlantic Standard (AST).

Sunrise/Sunset Average: 6:54 am to 6:21 pm

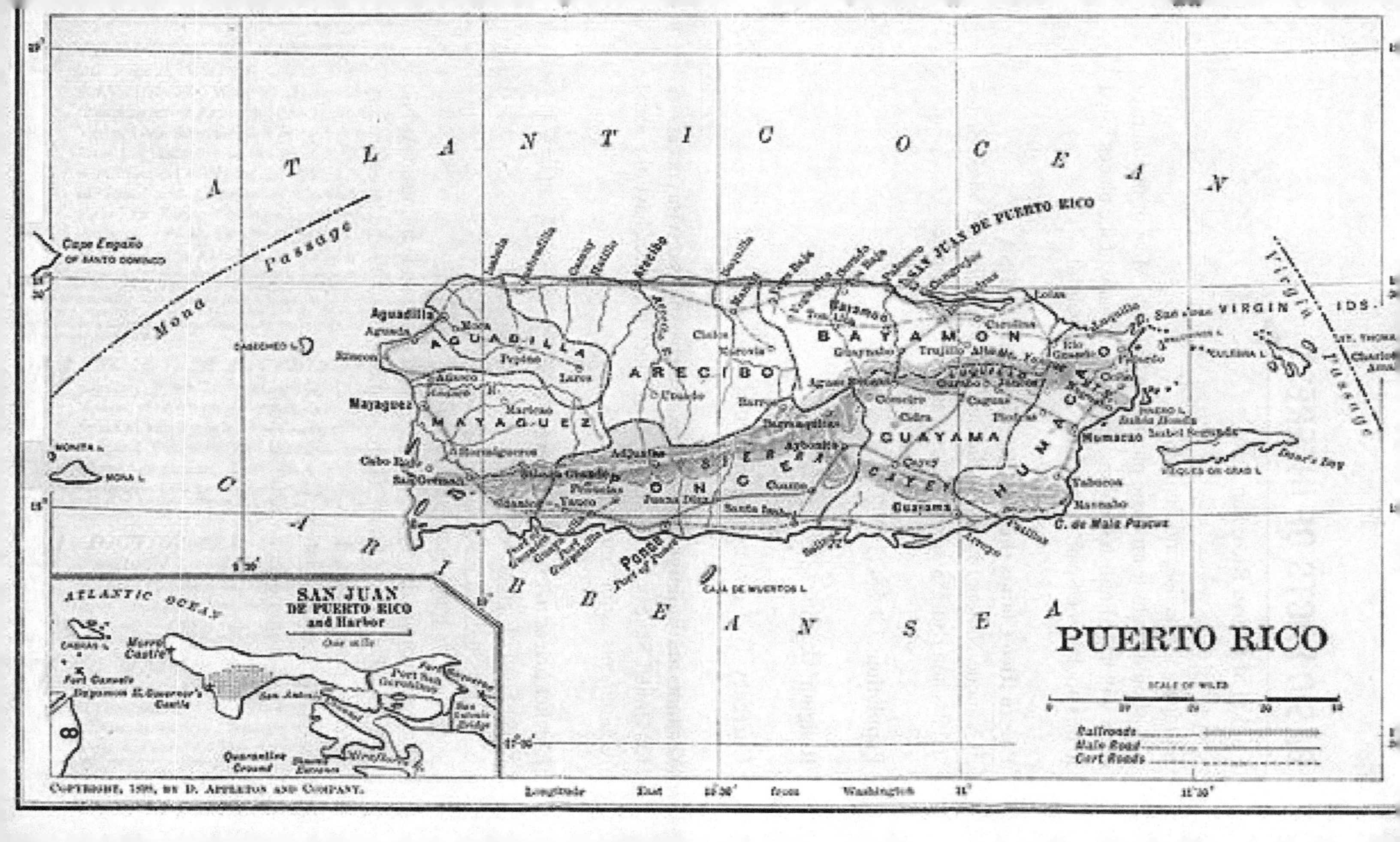

PUERTO RICO
ATLANTIC OCEAN
CARIBBEAN SEA
Mona Passage
Virgin Passage
VIRGIN IDS.
SAN JUAN DE PUERTO RICO
Cape Engaño OF SANTO DOMINGO
AGUADILLA
MAYAGUEZ
ARECIBO
BAYAMON
GUAYAMA
HUMACAO
SIERRA
Aguadilla
Mayaguez
Ponce
Arecibo
Guayama
Humacao
C. de Mala Pascua
CAJA DE MUERTOS I.
MONA I.
SAN JUAN DE PUERTO RICO and Harbor
ATLANTIC OCEAN
Morro Castle
SCALE OF MILES
Railroads
Carl Roads
Longitude
East
from
Washington
COPYRIGHT, 1899, BY D. APPLETON AND COMPANY.

BASIC FACTS OF INTEREST

Capital of Puerto Rico: San Juan

Languages: Spanish and English.
You should try to learn basic phrases in Spanish. Most of the touristy areas will have English speaking staff but for many of the places listed in this book some Spanish speaking could be helpful.

Puerto Rico Claims the Only Rainforest in the USA
El Yunque National Forest is the only rainforest in the United States and it's home to 183 animal species and 225 tree species

Population: 3,098,423 (2022 est.)

Religion: Catholic (85%)

Currency: United States dollar (USD)

Customs and Immigration: There are no passports or visas necessary for United States citizens. Citizens of other countries have the same requirements as for entering the USA.

Market prices to expect per person
Street Food / Budget meal: US $3-15
Moderate Sit down restaurant meal: US $15-30
Top-end restaurant meal: US $30 and up
Budget accommodation: US $40-75. We recommend renting an Airbnb with a kitchen to save funds. There are plenty of small and large grocery stores to purchase food.
Moderate accommodation: US $75-200
Top-end accommodation $200 and up

Transportation: You can get to Puerto Rico by air or by sea. We recommend that you rent a car from a major car rental company with an onsite airport location. Yes, there are Ubers available however you will need a rental to get to almost all of the places in this book. We recommend renting a small SUV if you can afford it to maximize the number of the places you can reach comfortably. Caution: DO NOT be fooled by the little known rental companies that shuttle you to an offsite location. This is an area where we recommend that you spend some of the money that you will save by reading this book. These places will be a nightmare featuring long lines and bad customer service. This is not a good way for you to start and/or end your epic vacation Right?!

There are no public transportation services outside of the metropolitan areas.

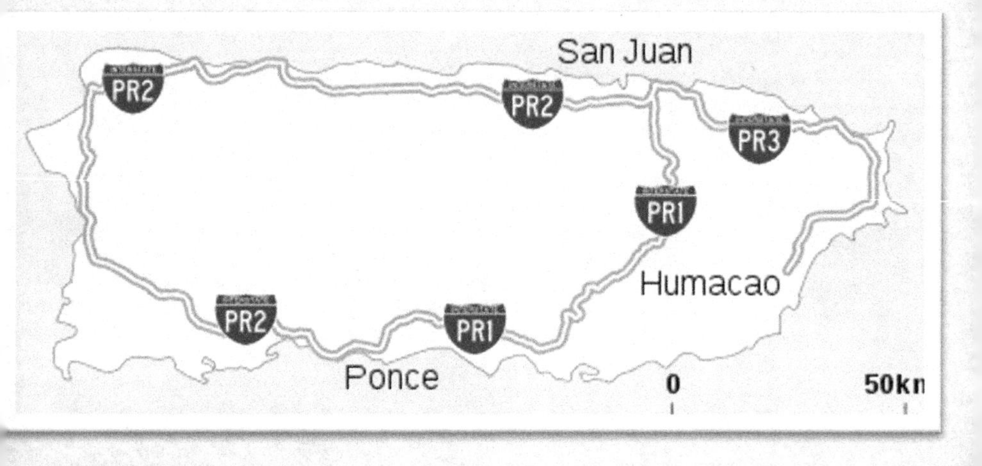

Medical / Hospitals:
The hospitals are rated as some of the greatest in the Caribbean. There are hospitals in all major cities.

Drinking Water: Deemed safe to drink as of 2021 data. Puerto Rico follows the same standards as the USA to sanitize water by following the EPA Safe Water Act.

There is a Forbidden Island

Desecheo Island, one of Puerto Rico's islands, is off-limits to visitors since it was used as a training and test field by the United States Navy. It still has explosives on location. Visitors can only visit Desecheo Island's coastline.

Driving: Driving is on the right-hand side of the road. All the same rules as any part of the United States except that the signs are in Spanish, the distance markers are in kilometers and the gas is sold in liters. Many roads are along the coastline with steep drops or may require driving on a possibly wet and/or muddy dirt road. Drive slowly and carefully.

NOT SO FUN FACT

Snake Invaders
There has been an invasive species of Boa Constrictor competing with native snakes. These snakes are an issue on mostly the western/northern portion of the island with Mayaguez as the epicenter. These boas have no natural predators to keep the population under control.

They have been seen all up and down the west and northern parts of the island especially in the forest/ forest edge and along roads.

"Stray" Animals
As of 2022, there are only five shelters housing stray dogs across all 78 municipalities in Puerto Rico. These shelters report a euthanasia rate of 94%. There are an estimated 500,000 stray dogs on the island. You will see them roaming all over the island, in our experience they are friendly. We had the pleasure of dogs and roosters joining us in our rental without an issue. But always use caution when approaching any animals.

If you are interested in helping these animals, consider supporting the Sato Project. The Sato Project has rescued over 5,500 dogs in Puerto Rico since 2011 and continues to bring light to the issue. Please visit www.thesatoproject.org for more information.

Covid travel Information:
For the most up to date information and requirements see the Puerto Rico travel safe website. As of 2022, the website address is https://www.travelsafe.pr.gov

PRO TIPS

Medical cannabis for travelers:

If you are already a Medical Cannabis USA Patient then your out-of-state medical card is accepted in Puerto Rico. However, you will need to visit a doctor in Puerto Rico to discuss your medical history.

Patients must be age 21 or over in order to apply for a medical marijuana card themselves. Anyone under 21 can have caregivers apply for them. Plan to pay a minimum of $125 to gain the right to purchase the following cannabis products while in Puerto Rico.

- Capsules or tablets
- Concentrates
- Edibles
- Oils
- Oral drops
- Oral inhalers
- Suppositories
- Topical ointments and creams
- Transdermal patches
- Vaping

Recreational cannabis is illegal & you can NOT purchase cannabis flower EVEN WITH a Medical License as it is strictly illegal.

Side note: As of 2022, anyone can purchase Delta 8 products found within smoke shops around the island.

Paid Tours?!?!

If you end up wanting to book a tour, please be aware of possible scams involving fake tours. Check reviews and make sure the name, address and phones #'s match the company you are trying to book with.

Locals

Puerto Ricans are generally known to be wonderfully warm and kind. For example, if you are eating and a local walks by you; you may hear them say "BUEN PROVECHO"; roughly meaning enjoy your meal. You can simply say Gracias or Thank you.

Mobile Phones

If you adventure into the central area of the island, you might lose your cell signal at some point.

Swimming in Ocean and Rip Tides

Rip tides are strong currents caused by tidal flow in a confined area. Many people drown every year due to getting trapped in rip tides. Always research if the beach you are heading to has rip currents and never swim alone. Even calm looking areas of water can have deadly hidden rip tides.

Cocktail anyone?

The legal drinking age in Puerto Rico is 18 years although some clubs may require you to be 21 to enter. You can purchase alcohol in bars, gas stations and even convenience stores.

FUN FACTS ABOUT PUERTO RICO

There are 3 Bioluminescent Lagoons

Bioluminescence is a biochemical emission of light by a living organism the dinoflagellates and it is quite a unique marvel in the world. You can find not only one, not two but three bioluminescent bays in Puerto Rico. The first is La Parguera in Lajas, Laguna Grande in Fajardo and then Mosquito Bay in Vieques Island. Unfortunately, it is believed that the populations of dinoflagellates had been damaged by chemicals such as sunscreen. This damage has caused the brightness of the first two bays to be diminished. However, Mosquito Bay in Vieques holds the Guinness Record for the brightest bioluminescent bay in the world and for its high concentration of dinoflagellate. swimming is not allowed.

The World's oldest living man

is Puerto Rican, Guinness World Records confirms that Emilio "Don Millo" Flores Márquez is the world's oldest living man at age 112.

OG Streets

Some of the streets have original cobblestones. You can still see some of the original ones in the streets of Old San Juan. There is a debate on if these stones are from the early 1600's or the late 1700's.

Oldest Carnival in the West Hemisphere

Historians believe that the Carnival in Ponce is one of the oldest in the Western Hemisphere. One of Puerto Rico's top festivities, the Ponce Carnival dates back to 1858 and it takes place every year one week before Ash Wednesday.

Largest Rum Distillery in the World

If you've ever tasted alcohol, then you have probably heard of Bacardí Rum. Bacardí originated in Cuba and established facilities in Puerto Rico in 1930. After the Cuban Revolution, Bacardí continued its operations in Cataño, Puerto Rico, where you can now find the largest distillery in the world.

Crime and Safety:

Puerto Rico is considered safe to visit (2022). It has a crime rate beneath many mainland USA cities. Just use common sense and keep your belongings close by.

LGBTQ2+ Travel

Puerto Rico is said to have some of the most progressive laws for and one of the most vibrant LGBTQ2+ communities in the Caribbean. Atlantic Beach - Condado Beach is a popular gay friendly beach in San Juan; great for gathering, relaxing and walking the shoreline with friends, family or lovers; not great for swimming as the currents are rough. San Juan has an annual pride festival the first weekend of June.

Puerto Rican Citizenship

Yes, Puerto Ricans can have two citizenships, even though they are citizens of one country. Puerto Rico has commonwealth status as it is neither a state nor an independent country.

The Supreme Court of Puerto Rico reaffirmed the standing existence of Puerto Rican citizenship in 1997. The government has granted Puerto Rican citizenship to anyone born in Puerto Rico and also to people who have at least one parent who was born in Puerto Rico.

The Islands Name

From Borikén to San Juan Bautista to Puerto Rico to Porto Rico back to Puerto Rico to Estado Libre Asociado de Puerto Rico / Commonwealth of Puerto Rico. Locals may call the island as Borinquén deriving from the original Borikén. Many Puerto Ricans are also called Boricuas.

Oldest residence

San Juan has the oldest remaining Spanish residence; Casa Blanca was intended to be the home of Ponce de Leon before he died; the ruins of the home are still on site. Currently, there is a small museum on site as well.

Puerto Ricans Don't Vote in US Elections

Puerto Ricans are US citizens but they can't vote in the US Presidential General Election or for the US Congress.

Modern Culture:

Culture is a series of visual manifestations & interactions with the environment that make a region and/or a group of people different from the rest of the world. Puerto Rican culture is complex and colorful. Puerto Ricans include a mix of Taino, Spanish, African and American races. Approximately 60% of the those living in Puerto Rico identify as white, about 30% identify as other race and about 12% as black. The epicenter of the black community and culture in Puerto Rico is in the town of Loíza about 40 minutes from San Juan where bout 60% of the residents identify as black.

Many cultures contribute to the awesomeness of Puerto Rico. During the Spanish invasion they took Taíno women as brides. The Spanish needed a large labor force and they replied heavily on African slaves, Chinese immigrants, Italians, French, German and even individuals from Lebanon. Most recently many Cubans and people from the Dominican Republic have made Puerto Rico home. These influences made this marvelous island the paradise you see today.

22

FOOD!

10 Legit Flavor Packed & Low-Cost Eats and Drinks to seek out throughout all of your adventures

While this is a hidden gems book of activities and things to do and see; ALL Epic vacations require Epic food! So of course, we couldn't leave food out of this book.

Here is a list of 10 quintessential Puerto Rican foods you must try during your travels. If this cuisine is not familiar to you; just go for it. Try new things! We promise you that they are ALL delectable and modestly priced. There are so many great places to eat in Puerto Rico. Just about anywhere you stop you will find finger-lickingly good food. So instead of listing specific restaurant recommendations we have compiled a list of must try foods that you could be able to find at any establishment you go to.

If you would like a sure fire way to acquire many Puerto Rican treats all in one place: Piñones is Puerto Rico's fritter capital and you'll find dozens of Puerto Ricans in every kiosk enjoying traditional Puerto Rican foods like alcapurrias and bacalaítos. Piñones is also famous for its beach boardwalk and La Pocita de Piñones, a family-friendly beach.

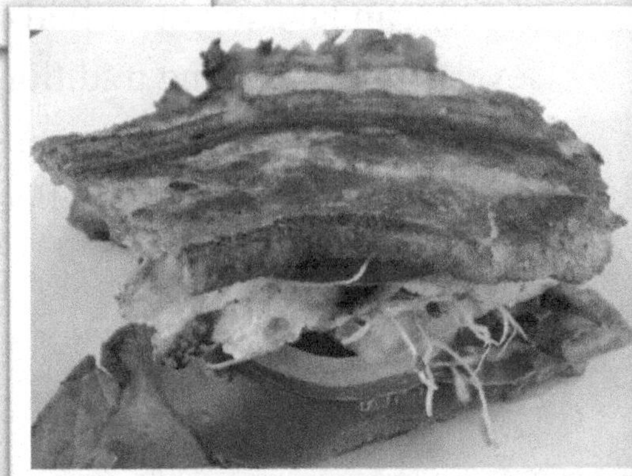

Alcapurrias

A massively popular Puerto Rican street food. A mouthwatering handheld fritter consisting of green bananas and yautía (taro root), stuffed with a savory meat usually ground beef encased in masa (dough) & fried to perfection. Taste profile: These should be crunchy on the outside and spicy, sweet and doughy on the inside.

Arroz con Gandules

One of the island's national dishes; Arroz con Gandules is a combination of rice, pigeon peas, olives and pork. Cooked with sofrito. Pigeon Pea are a bean native to Africa. Taste Profile: Fluffy soft flavored rice with the saltiness from olives and a "nutty" taste of pigeon peas.

Bacalaitos

Bacalaitos are a fried salt cod "fritter" made with finely chopped onions, red pepper, cilantro, and a touch of oregano. Taste profile: Light, fluffy with savory flavor from fresh herbs.

Jibarito

a sandwich made with flattened, fried green plantains instead of bread, aioli (garlic-flavored mayonnaise), and a filling that typically includes meat, cheese, lettuce and tomato. Taste profile: The plantain "bread" is similar to a fried potato but sweeter.

Empanadas vs. empanadillas vs. pastelillos

Is the same item by our standards. This treat is made with fried flaky pie dough typically filled with ground beef, peppers and olives. These treats are so versatile and can be filled with either savory or sweet items. Taste Profile: Tender flaky pastry with a nice saltiness and savory fillings.

The Piña Colada

Is the official drink of the island and was invented in Puerto Rico. This tasty treat is made with pineapple juice, rum, and cream of coconut. Taste Profile: Rich, refreshing and sweet with the consistency of a fruit smoothie.

Pasteles

This tasty delight is made with green plantain masa dough that is filled with a savory pork and adobo mix wrapped in green banana leaves and boiled. Taste Profile: Tender starchy texture similar to a tamale.

Pernil Asado

A caramelized slow cooked pork shoulder marinated in citrus juices and garlic usually made for holiday feasts. Taste Profile: Ideally made with crispy skin and the taste of cilantro and garlic.

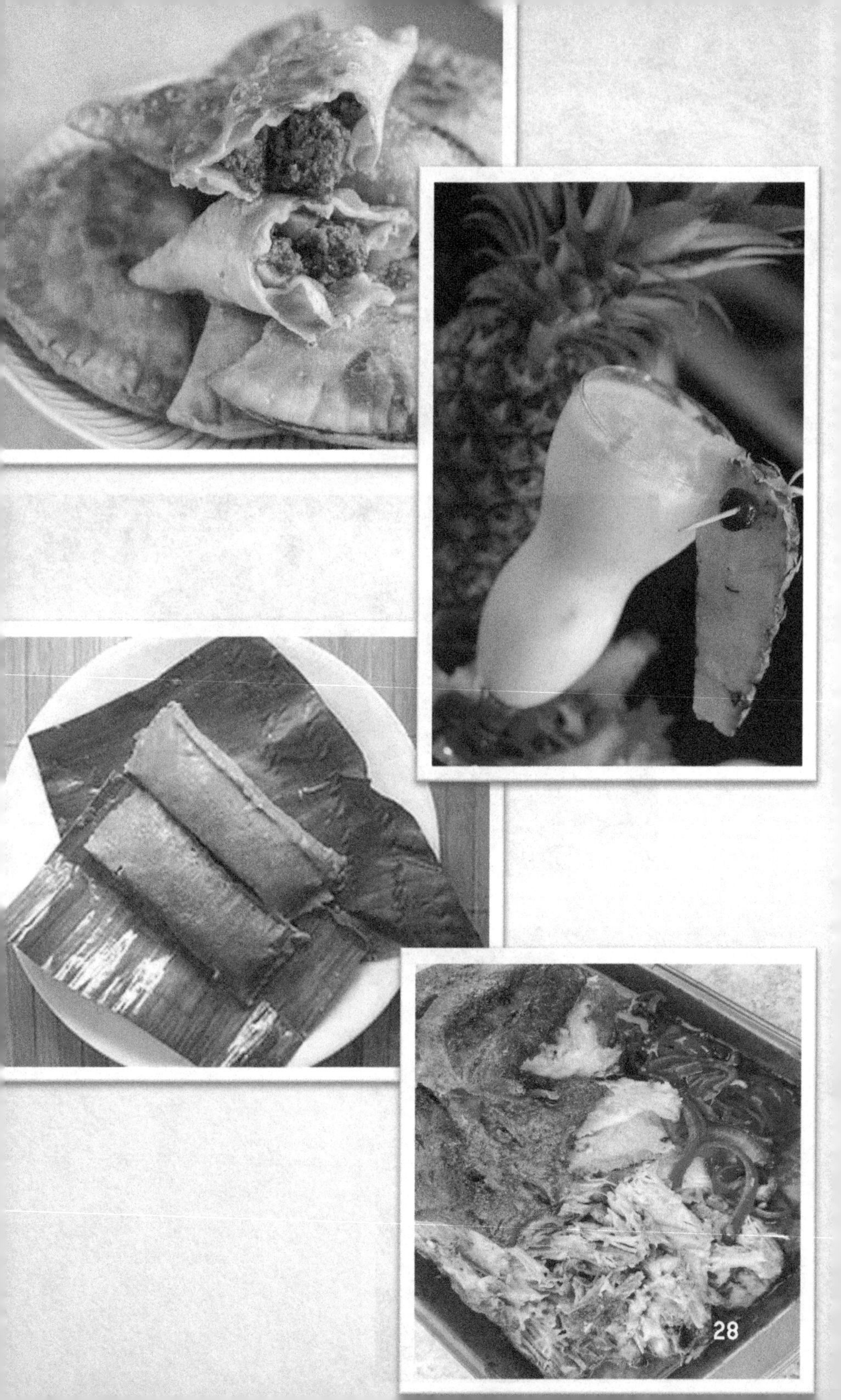

Coquito

Coquito meaning "Little Coconut" in Spanish is a traditional Christmas drink that originated in Puerto Rico. The coconut-based alcoholic beverage is similar to eggnog, and is sometimes referred to as Puerto Rican Eggnog. The mixed drink is made with Puerto Rican rum, coconut milk, cream of coconut, sweetened condensed milk, vanilla, nutmeg, clove, and cinnamon. Taste Profile: Creamy and sweet with a heavy focus on the coconut flavor.

Mofongo

Mofongo is a popular dish made from fried green plantains or fried yuca, seasoned with garlic, olive oil and pork cracklings, then mashed. Can be served with various proteins. Taste Profile: The plantain base is similar to a very thick and hearty mashed potato with a sweet taste.

Bonus tempting treat to try:

Arroz con Dulce

Arroz con Dulce roughly translated to Sweetened Rice.
More easily obtainable during holiday times, look for it from around Thanksgiving to New Years.
This yummy dessert is a sweet rice pudding mixed with coconut and raisins. This delectable treat is far from bland with the addition of spices such as cinnamon, ginger, and cloves. Taste Profile: Tender grains of rice with a texture similar to a "loose" oatmeal.

Water & Natural World Wonder Gems

LA PLAYUELA BEACH

sometimes called Playa Sucia

Clear Water // Spectacular Views

In our opinion, this is Puerto Rico's most beautiful beach. This is an expansive crescent moon shaped remote beach with clear blue waters. We love this location because of all the "take your breath away" moments you will find. After visiting the Cabo Rojo Lighthouse AKA Faro Los Morrillos de Cabo Rojo, you can spend the day at (in our opinion) the best beach in Puerto Rico.

You can find shady and sunny spots to chill and clear water to swim. After swimming you can climb the surrounding cliffs and explore the trails.

Excellent location for family photos.

There were some areas with seaweed along the shore but many large clear areas are available to swim. The waves on this beach can vary from calm and flat to small waves. This is a remote beach, so no lifeguards, equipment rentals, food vendors, or restrooms. Bring your own chairs, blankets and coolers.

Pro Tip: Call the Faro Los Morrillos lighthouse at 787-851-4700 to confirm if the area is open.

Whereabouts: About 3 hours from San Juan. Southwest tip of the island.
Address: PR-301, Cabo Rojo, PR, 00623

The Way: Drive all the way to the end of Route 301. Make a left when you arrive at the lighthouse parking lot. You can walk down to this beach from the Cabo Rojo Lighthouse if you like. As you continue, you will pass eerily beautiful salt flats. This road is WILD and you may question several times if this is the right way as you will find massive potholes in the road. You will have to weave in and out so drive slowly. Not recommended for compact vehicles.

There are two parking areas; the first parking area will be about a 5-10 minute walk to the beach but you will walk along the beautiful wetlands. To get to the 2nd and closer parking area continue to drive down the dirt road path. It looks like a just walking path but if you continue to drive down you will find additional much closer parking. The park rangers will close the road if the parking is full.

Activity Expense: FREE

Best time to visit: Best parking before 9 a.m as you will be turned away if the parking is full; park rangers will close the area at dusk.

CRASH BOAT BEACH

AKA PLAYA CRASHBOAT

Snorkel // Calm swimming // Locals love it

Located on a former Air Force base marina where "crashboats" were launched from here to retrieve planes that crashed during training missions. This is a large and popular beach known for smooth sand & calm clear water. Perfect location for swimming and snorkeling with seahorses, frogs, schools of fish, octopi, lionfish and stingrays. Known as a festive beach as you will hear music and see both locals and tourists together eating and enjoying life.

It is important to describe the two distinct areas of the beach, the paid parking side and the free parking side.

When you first arrive at the beach area, the first parking area down the hill is the paid parking side of the beach. This part of the beach is cleaned by staff and also has restrooms although they unfortunately are not known to be cleaned very well; they will work for emergency bathroom situations. There is also a designated swimming only area in this part; which is perfect for children as you will not have to be concerned with active boats or jet skis coming too close. There are shady areas as well by the rocks with a few picnic tables close by. This side is a sunbathers dream with big open areas to lay.

Continue straight to get to the free parking side. You will go over a waterway; continue until you arrive at the free parking area. This area is not cleaned by staff as often and there is no designated swimming only area but this is a popular place to swim.

There are food, drink and craft vendors as well as an equipment rental shop to rent snorkel gear, stand up paddle boards & kayaks; guided tours are also available.
The fishing pier in this area is the best snorkel spot at this beach.
Contact West Paradise Water Sports at 787-891-8602 or 787-692-5538 in advance if you plan on renting equipment. This area is also popular with divers.

Whereabouts: Northwest side of the island; about 2 hours from San Juan. In the town of Aguadilla, PR, 00603

The Way: From the San Juan area, take Route 22 west to Route 2 west. Turn right onto Road 107, and then left onto Road 458. Follow the signs.

Activity Expense: Free parking on the side of the street where the food carts are located; be careful to not park on any yellow lines or after the wooden observation deck as this area is known for having expensive parking tickets. There are also paid parking lots (about $5) on the other side of the street.

Best time to visit: open from 9:00 a.m. to 5:00 p.m. This is a very popular beach so plan to arrive before 10:00 a.m for the best parking and beach location. Least crowded before noon on weekdays.

DOÑA JUANA WATERFALL

AKA Catarata Chorro de Doña Juana

Waterfall // Photo Op

Details: A delightfully beautiful roadside waterfall with a small swimming hole. Excellent setting for selfies and family photos. Perfect for diving in for a quick dip to cool off if you can brave the rocks leading down to the water. Parking can be difficult depending on the time of day, if possible arrive early. Be extra careful when crossing this street to reach the waterfall.

Whereabouts: The center of the island; about 2 hours from San Juan in the town of Orocovis
Address: PR-149 Orocovis, PR, 00766

The Way: Get on Hwy 1 S/PR-1 S in Santurce from PR-26, Take Autop. José de Diego/PR-22 W to PR-149 in Manatí. Take exit 48 from Autop. José de Diego/PR-22 W, Drive to PR-149 in Orocovis.
The waterfall will be located between mile markers KM 42.1 and 42.3 on PR-149. Look for areas to pull off on the side of the road both before and after the waterfall.

Activity Expense: FREE

Best Time to Visit: early morning or before dusk.

CAMUY RIVER CAVE PARK

AKA Parque Nacional de las Cavernas del Rio Camuy

Day Trip // Family Friendly

Details:
Magical natural limestone underground caverns shaped by the 3rd largest underground waterway on earth called the Río Camuy aka Camuy River. There are many attractions at this park with the main attraction being Cueva Clara having ceilings that top over 170 feet high. See stalagmites and stalactites that are estimated to be over 45 million years of age including the largest in all of Puerto Rico.
Open to the public for 1 mile walking audio tours. 1.5 hour group walking tour with audio headset; tours are offered in both English and Spanish. Difficulty of walking is rated as moderate to difficult. You are advised to wear closed toe non-slip footwear.
For reservations: email mgonzalez@jca.pr.gov but reservations are not required. You can also call 787-898-3136, 787-898-3100, 787-999-2200 ext 3474 for details and to ensure wheelchair and stroller accessibility.

Whereabouts: Northwest part of the island - 1.5 hours from San Juan in the town of Quebrada - Highway 129 - km. 18.9 Quebrada, 00669 Puerto Rico

The Way: on PR road 22 take exit 77B and connect with highway 129 towards Lares, Follow PR-129 to Parque De Las Cavernas Del Río Camuy in Camuy, Merge onto Carr. Mariana Bracetti/PR-129 - the park will be on your left.

Activity Expense: $19 adults, $13 ages 4-12 and seniors $9

Best time to visit: Wednesday - Sunday 10:30 a.m. to 5 p.m. Arrive by 3:30pm

FINCA EL GIRASOL

AKA The Sunflower Farm

Photo Ops // Family & Pet Friendly

Details: A highly rated sunflower farm; great for a quick family adventure or fun date. This small family run farm has a shop with a variety of sunflowers and fruit for sale. Great place for wedding proposals and family photo shoots. Call 939-402-7967 for details; message is in Spanish however you can text them any questions to this number. They can be found on facebook as well. Beware of local honeybees around the farm if allergic.

Whereabouts: Southwestern coast of the island; about 2 hours from San Juan.
Address: PR 116 Guanica 00653

Best time to visit: Open Friday, Saturday and Sunday; 7:00 a.m. to 6 p.m.

The Way: Take Hwy 1 S/PR-1 S; Take the exit onto Autop. José de Diego/Expreso José de Diego/PR-22 W; Take exit 2A on the left for Puerto Rico 18 S toward Río Piedras/Cupey/Caguas; Keep left to stay on Autop. Luis A. Ferré/PR-52; Continue onto Carr Puerto Rico 2 O/PR-2 W; Take the exit toward PR-116. Farm is about 1 mile from the exit.

Activity Expense: $2 per person. Entry fee is for parking and to walk the fields; take home flowers are extra.

GUÁNICA STATE FOREST - BOSQUE ESTATAL DE GUÁNICA

AKA Guánica Dry Forest

Water Views // Ruins and Hiking

Whereabouts: Southwest side of Puerto Rico - 2 hours from San Juan and 30 minutes from Ponce

The Way: Follow Route 116 until you reach Route 334. Take exit toward Bosque Estatal de Guánica. You may not see many signs to this forest while you are on the way but if you follow Rt 334 up and to the left you will eventually see the Welcome to the forest sign and the parking area.

Details:
There are many popular rainforests in Puerto Rico to visit but this area is known as the "Paradise of the Eternal Summer". This is a lesser familiar hidden gem forest with not only breathtaking trails but an historical fort, natural caves, birds galore and thrilling coastline views.

If large crowds are an issue this will suit your needs.

Guánica State Forest is what is known as a dry forest and is actually one of the largest tropical dry coastal forests in the world. This forest receives only 30 inches of rain per year on average; compare this to the 200+ inches of rain in Puerto Rico's El Yunque forest area. You will find cactuses and other dry weather flora thriving here.

Restrooms available close to the information center.

Some things to do while here:
A popular activity is to see the ruins of Fort Fuerto Capron via a "easy" 6 mile hike leading to spectacular water views of Guánica Bay and this historic fort. The fort was first built in the 16th century. The trail to the fort is composed of packed dirt and rock creating a road that is moderately easy to walk on if you can manage going up some hills. This walk is not shaded so bring sunscreen, a hat and water.

We understand that this hike would not be "easy" for everyone but this would be similar to walking 6 miles on a dirt road.

How to find the fort: Once on the hiking trail, you will eventually come to a "Y" on the trail. You want to go uphill and to the left and not downhill to the right.

Obtain a good trail map to help.
Pro Tip: If you just want to see the fort you can with a short 10 minute walk by parking on the road at RT 333 at 17.9545296,-66.904332 and follow the path up.

Shorter hikes to magical views and a hidden beach on the Ballena Trail or you can see natural caves and coastline views on the Cueva Trail. Again a good trail map can help with this.

This is also a birdwatchers heaven with over 130 different birds found here.

Activity Expense: Free entrance and parking

Best time to visit: Closed Mondays - open from 8:30 am to 4:00 pm; call 787-772-2009 or 787-821-5706 to confirm details. The Visitor Center is closed for lunch from 12:00 p.m. to 1:00 p.m.

MAR CHIQUITA

AKA Little Sea

Details: This jewel is a picture perfect natural pool of water that is partially separated and protected from the Atlantic Ocean by a wall of rock. You can swim, snorkel and sunbath here. If the waves are too big for swimming; skip the water and explore the rock formations; take unbelievable photos and explore. One word of caution; there is a noted undertow depending on the tide and size of waves entering the cove. There are no lifeguards on site and we recommend wearing water shoes as there may be slippery rocks. Food vendors should arrive in the early afternoon, this is a great opportunity to try some of the foods listed in this guide. May have a portable potty in the parking lot but no official restroom or showers. No shady areas around but you could be able to rent an umbrella from a local vendor.

Whereabouts: North side of the island centrally located by the city of Manati. About 45 minutes from San Juan.

The Way: Drive on Route 22 to exit 46 to Route 686 north. Drive on Route 685 west to Route to Route 648 north and travel to the end of the road.

Activity Expense: Beach and Parking is Free

Best time to visit: Early morning before 11 a.m. for smaller waves & the water is generally calmer in the summer months but if you are looking for less crowds the winter months are for you.

SEVEN SEAS BEACH

AKA Playa Seven Seas

Swim // Snorkel and Views

The Way: Take Route 3 in Fajardo to Route 194. You will pass the El Conquistador Resort and Route 194 becomes Route 987. Take 987 until you reach Seven Seas Beach on your left.

Activity Expense: $5 parking; gazebos for rent by the day about $30, overnight stay campsites $10 per person with 2 night rental required. Book campsites in advance by calling Parques Nacionales at 787-622-5200.
Bathroom with showers available for $1.
Umbrellas, tables and beach chairs also available for rent

Best time to visit: before 5 p.m. to use facilities. Winter is less crowded

Details: Swim, Snorkel, Eat or spend the night on the beach. Seven Seas Beach is one of the best overall beaches in Puerto Rico. Featuring beautiful views, sunny and shaded areas, calm waters, great swimming & snorkeling as well as facilities to make your day more comfortable. Family friendly as this is a rare beach with lifeguards and security on the lookout. Restaurant should be open on the weekends. We recommend water shoes as most of the entrance to the water is hard stone and maybe hard to walk on.

Pro Tip: Looking for a much more private paradise spot. There are TWO Secret Hidden Beaches within a 15-20 minute walk; Colorá Beach also known as Red Beach due to the reddish color sand and Playa Escondida.
Both are known for their swimmable shallow clear waters and beautiful views.
The way to the hidden beaches: Facing the water of Seven Sea Beach, walk all the way to the left until you reach the end of the beach; you will see a path. You will walk through a beach forest. You will see a path between the mangroves that will guide you. You may smell some rotting vegetation but keep walking. It takes around 15-20 minutes to reach either secret beach.
Once you start on the path take the first right turn and follow to the right for Playa Colorá or go straight for Playa Escondida. You will need to bring everything you need with you as there are no vendors or facilities.

Whereabouts: Eastern Side of the Island about an hour from San Juan in the town of Fajardo

CASCADA GOZALANDIA

AKA Gozalandia Waterfall

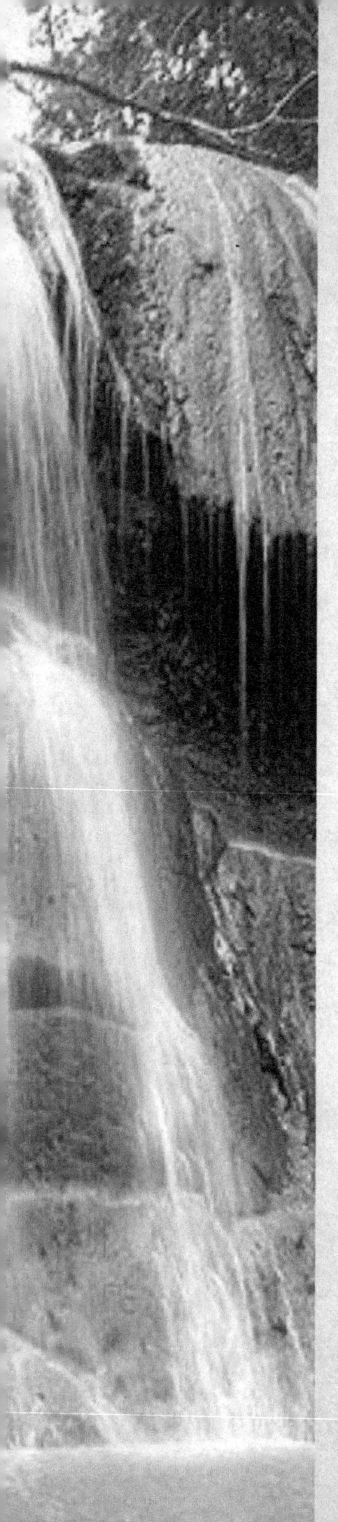

Whereabouts: Western Side of the Island in the San Sebastian area about 2 hours from San Juan

Details: Couple of waterfalls, swimming holes and a rope swing.
Perfect to cool off by swimming on a hot sunny day and beautiful to view on any day. Well paved 4 minute walk down to this natural 60 foot tall waterfall and swimming hole has been seen in feature films. The swimming holes are said to be 20 to 30 feet deep. You will have access to a restroom that is located close to the restaurant.
You will take stairs down to the waterfall from the parking lot.
The steps and path down to the waterfall may be slippery so wear appropriate shoes and swim suit if needed.
Are you the adventurous type? There is an upper waterfall if you follow the cement walkway along the river. This area could be less crowded. There will be many little pools to swim in along the path. Continue along the path for a total of about a 10-15 minute walk. You should find a rope swing on the left side of this waterfall.

The Way: Route 111 in San Sebastian turns north onto Route 446. You will see a large bridge on the right; continue across the bridge; follow the road for about a ½ mile. Look for a large gate on the left. A sign will say Sha's Restaurant & Bar.

Activity Expense: $10 cash for parking

Best time to visit: 10 a.m. to 6 p.m.

CUEVA DEL VIENTO

AKA Cave of the Winds

Details: You will walk deep inside the Guajataca Forest to get to the cave. Park employees should be available to provide maps and directions. You will need to take trail number #1 which is also the beginning of the Interpretative Trail to reach the cave. At the beginning of the trail you will see a trail marker for the Observation Tower on the right. Follow the path for trail #1. When you arrive at the cave; you will see a sign that says "Danger Zone". You have to go down 40 stairs and some of the stairs going into the cave have dry rotted so use caution. Not recommended for young children. This adventure is for those with enough strength and endurance to make about a 2.5 mile or 1 ½ - 2 hour walk roundtrip.

You can also do some nice birdwatching.

Call the Bosque Estatal de Guajataca at 787-872-1045 or email bosquedeguajataca@gmail.com for up to date information. Wear shoes appropriate for trail walking. You will need to bring your own flashlight.

Whereabouts: Northwestern part of the Island in the Isabela area - Guajataca Forest - about 2 hours from San Juan. The forest information office is located at Route 446 KM 11. Office is open Tuesday to Sunday from 10 a.m to 4:00 p.m.

The Way: Take Route 2 to about KM 108 and turn onto Route 446. Follow Route 446 into the forest. There is a forest information office and parking around KM 11 on Route 446.

Activity Expense: Free

Best time to visit: Open Daily 9 a.m. to 5 p.m.

EL CHARCO AZUL

AKA Blue Pond

Whereabouts: Southeastern part of the island - town of Patillas in the Carite Forest

The Way: from the San Juan area, take Route 18/52 south to exit 32 (the Guavate exit) to Route 184. Follow Route 184 through Guavate and the forest for 15 minutes or so. Make sure to stay on Route 184 until you get to the Charco Azul Recreation Area at KM 17.8.
From the parking area walk across the street and follow the path until you see the ruins of the restrooms. You will walk about ½ mile to the pool. .

Activity Expense: FREE

Best time to visit: Weekdays are least crowded.

Details: A natural swimming pool and cave/rock formations in the middle of the Carite Forest. This is a beautiful little fresh water swimming hole about 40 feet across. There is also a super cute small waterfall on site. It will take about a 10 minute walk to reach the natural blue pool. No lifeguards onsite and also there are no restrooms as they were destroyed by Hurricane Maria. Wear water shoes as there are some rocks on the bottom of the pool..

There are also many companies you can find that offer guided tours to this location.

Not recommended for children or elderly as this could be a difficult walk. Arrive early as parking can be tough at times. Call 787-747-4545 for details.

EL FARO LOS MORRILLOS DE CABO ROJO

AKA Cabo Rojo Lighthouse & Playa Sucia / La Playuela Beach

Details: The Cabo Rojo Lighthouse looms over the beautiful waters of the Caribbean. Los Morrillos was completed in 1882 and is regarded as one the the most beautiful of Puerto Rico's fourteen lighthouses. It was used to guide ships through the Mona Passage. This Spanish colonial style structure rests on a 200 foot high limestone cliff and provides nearly 360-degree views of the Caribbean Sea. The road to the lighthouse is in need of maintenance so please drive carefully. Recommend to wear sturdy walking shoes as the path to the lighthouse is rocky. The walk to reach the lighthouse is about .75 miles each way. It will be about a 10-15 minute walk to the lighthouse.

Whereabouts: Southwest part of the island. Southeastern point of Cabo Rojo.
About 3 hours from San Juan on the Morrillos Peninsula.
Cabo Rojo, PR, 00623

The Way:
From Cabo Rojo Take PR-100 to PR-301. Follow 301 PR to the end

Activity Expense: Free

Best time to visit: 9:00 a.m. - 5:30 p.m.; Tours may be available inside of the lighthouse but call 787-851-1025 or 787-255-1560 if you plan to go inside as it may be closed at unknown times. In our opinion, the views and visit are still worthwhile even if you can not see the inside.

COAMO THERMAL HOT SPRINGS

AKA Aguas Termales de Coamo

AKA Baños de Coamo

Hot Tub // Relaxing // Fountain of Youth

Details: Come soak in mineral waters that Juan Ponce de León thought of as the "fountain of youth". Locals have used the spring water to help with diabetes, gout, circulation/respiratory issues as well as joint pain. There are two natural thermal spring pools with an average temperature of 109 fahrenheit; the water is naturally heated by an inactive volcano. The perfect combination of convenience meets raw nature.

Restrooms and changing rooms are available; bring your own towel but some towels may be available for a fee. You must rinse off in the showers before entering either pool.

It is recommended that you stay for only about 10-15 minutes but definitely no more than 20 minutes per session in the hot pools due to the high temperatures and the associated health risks.

Seating is available for relaxing in between your soaking sessions.

Call 787-825-6668 or email aguastermalescoamo@gmail.com for more details.

Whereabouts: Southern center of the island between Ponce and Caguas
About 1 1/2 hours to drive from San Juan
Address: Highway 546 at Km 1.7
Coamo, PR, 00769

The Way: from the San Juan area, take Route 52 South to exit 76. Take highway 153 North to Highway 546. Take Highway 546 all the way to the end.

Activity Expense: $5 for adults and $4 for children & seniors for access to pools; free parking

Best time to visit: Everyday 6 a.m. to 9 p.m. Busiest times are noon to 3 p.m. daily and all day saturday.

JARDIN BOTANICO Y CULTURAL WILLIAM MIRANDA MARIN GARDENS

AKA The William Miranda Marín Botanical and Cultural Garden

Gardens // Educational Tour // Paddle Boats

Details: Identify diverse native fauna and flora on beautifully manicured easy to walk trails. See artwork, artifacts and monuments encompassing the history of Puerto Rico. Learn about Taíno, African and Spanish influence on the area. The gardens sit on the remains of the old sugarcane factory Ingenio Azucar San Jose.

Arrange a guided tour or sign up for an educational workshop.

Bring good walking shoes as you will want to spend hours exploring everything the gardens have to offer.

Book tours in advance by calling 787-653-0470, 787-653-0469 or email info@jardinbotanicoycultural.org. You will see over 36 species of native and endemic trees, an indigenous taino public art project, 15 species of Cagüeño trees, 50 species of native and foreign fruit trees, wood carvings, bamboos, aquatic plants with tropical fish, hydroponics and butterflies. You will also get to see ruins of the old sugar mill. This is also a great place to purchase some of the Puerto Rican Foods listed in this book. Paddle boats may be available for rent to use on a small lake located on the property.

Whereabouts: Eastern side of the Island in the city of Caguas - Turabo Valley about 30 minute drive from San Juan
Address: Carr. # 156 Km. 56.5 Bo. Canabon, Caguas, Puerto Rico 00727

The Way: take road 156 towards Aguas Buena

Activity Expense: Unguided tour: Free
Guided Tours Adults (over 12 years old): $5.00, Children (2 to 12 years old): $3.00, Seniors 60+: $4.00

Best time to visit: Wednesday to Friday from 10:00 a.m. to 3:00 p.m. and Saturday and Sunday 10:00 a.m. to 4:00 p.m.

Cultural & Historical Gems

YOKAHÚ OBSERVATION TOWER

AKA Torre Yokahú in the El Yunque National Forest

Rainforest Views // Family Friendly // Alien Movie Film Area

Details: This is a popular 75 foot tall sixty year old observation tower featuring sweeping views of dense rainforest, the town of Luquillo and the surrounding coastline. Relatively easy walk of about 100 steps to get to the top for a view as pretty as a picture. These are the views you traveled all this way for! It is even possible to see the Virgin Islands on a cloudless day. A paved path makes this an easy walk for most individuals from the parking lot. Plan for about a 30 minute visit. You will need to make reservations for entry to the national park where the tower is located about 3-4 weeks in advance of your visit. This tower is just one of many locations to check out during your 3 hour El Yunque National Forest park pass. After you check out the tower you can experience so many other things including waterfalls, hiking trails, and swimming. We definitely recommend that you research all the activities available at this famous state forest. You can make reservations online at www.recreation.gov/ticket/facility/300017. Call 787-888-1880 for details.

Whereabouts: about 50 minutes from San Juan, Northeast side of the Island in the El Yunque National Forest
Address: Road 191 km 8.8

The Way: via Expreso Román Baldorioty de Castro/PR-26 and Autop. Roberto Sánchez Vilella/PR-66, Continue to Santurce, Head north on Calle Gral. Pershing toward P.º Covadonga/PR-38, Turn right onto P.º Covadonga/PR-38
Slight right onto Av. de la Constitución/PR-25/PR-26, Continue to follow PR-26
Turn left,Follow Expreso Román Baldorioty de Castro/PR-26 and Autop. Roberto Sánchez Vilella/PR-66 to PR-3 S/PRI-3 S in Río Grande. Exit from Autop. Roberto Sánchez Vilella/PR-66, Continue onto Expreso Román Baldorioty de Castro/PR-26

Continue straight onto Autop. Roberto Sánchez Vilella/PR-66
Continue straight to stay on Autop. Roberto Sánchez Vilella/PR-66
Toll road
Exit onto PR-3 S/PRI-3 S
Toll road,Merge onto PR-3 S/PRI-3 S
Keep right to stay on PR-3 S/PRI-3 S,Drive to PR-191
Turn right onto Cll Triunfo/PR-191
Turn right onto Cll Principal/PR-191/PR-955
Turn left onto PR-191

Activity Expense: $2.00 per person, must make a reservation for entry to the El Yunque National Forest to reach the tower. You can book entry tickets for 3 hour sessions from either 8:00 a.m. to 11:00 a.m. or 12:00 p.m. to 3:00 p.m.

Best Time to Visit: 9:00 a.m. to 4:00 p.m.

HACIENDA POMARROSA

History // Coffee // Amazing Views

Details: Tour of a family owned working coffee farm and factory. This is a 2 hour English speaking walking tour where you will learn the history of coffee in the Caribbean and the cultivation process used to create their delicious coffee from seed to cup. You can also view antique equipment used for coffee processing. If you are truly obsessed with coffee, ask them (in advance) about the full day coffee related workshops. There is a cafe on site to purchase the farm's coffee along with light snacks. You can extend your stay overnight in one of their gorgeous Villa rooms. All tours include a cup of coffee & homemade banana bread.

Tours and visits to the farm require a reservation by calling 787-844-3541 between the hours between 9:00 a.m. and 6:00 p.m. or 787-460-8934 for additional assistance.
Email address is info@pomarrosacoffeelodge.com.

It is recommended that you wear closed shoes and long sleeved shirts and pants for the tour.

Whereabouts: About 2 hours from San Juan - Western Center of the Island -
Address: 107 Carr. 511 Esq. Carr. 143 Barrio Anón, Sector Hogares Seguros, Puerto Rico 00731

The Way: From San Juan connect with highway 52 to Ponce via Caguas and take the exit at 98A – Ponce Norte/Adjuntas.
On highway 10 North (Norte) After 3.9 miles turn off to the right.
After 10.1 miles at km 24.2 turn right on to the Panoramic Highway traveling eastbound towards Barranquitas/Jayuya. There is only one road turning to the right.
After a short while, look for road sign 143. Make sure to stay on 143 until you reach road 511 at km 12.8; turn right on to 511. Drive 1/3 of a mile and you will see the entrance to the farm on the left: Pomarrosa Café Gourmet

Activity Expense: $20.00 all adults & $10.00 children under 10 years old

Best time to visit: Coffee Tours run once at day Mondays to Saturdays at 11:00 a.m with advanced reservations only

MUSEOS EL CEMI & CASA CANALES

AKA Nemesio Canales House

Details: Two attractions at one location. The first is the museum, El Cemi. The museum is a superb place to enjoy the tranquil ambience of the location while learning about the Taíno culture and customs. You will learn about many ancient religious artifacts.

The second is a museum to honor the town founders; the Canales family who were a prominent political family on the island. The house was the central location for a Nationalist Party uprising in the 1950's.
This attraction has easy parking and is considered an easy walk by many.
After your visit, you can also see authentic Taíno petroglyphs by going down Route 144 to La Piedra Escrita. You will find a boulder in the middle of Río Saliente with the art. Call 939-268-1910 or email tucentrojayuya@gmail.com for details.

Whereabouts: Puerto Rico in La Cordillera Central mountain range
Address: Rd. 144, km 9.3 Bo. Coabey, Jayuya, PR 00664

The Way: From Route 149, turn left on Route 144 and take it to KM 9.3. You will be able to see the El Cemi Museum and police station from the road.

Activity Expense: Adult $2 Children $1 for both museums

Best time to visit: 10:00 a.m. to 3:30 p.m.; closed for lunch from 12:30 p.m. to 1 p.m.

HACIENDA BUENA VISTA - PONCE COFFEE PLANTATION & MUSEUM

Coffee Lover // History

Details: This 87 acre plantation/museum complex shows the pinnacle of Puerto Rican coffee making and technology of the mid 19th and early 20th century. This complex once produced and exported 10,000 pounds of coffee per year.

Tour guides are known to be especially knowledgeable and dedicated to preserving history and culture of the Hacienda Buena Vista. This location is managed by Para La Naturaleza; a non-profit focused on preserving landmarks all over Puerto Rico. To visit the museum / plantation, you must make reservations in advance either online or by phone. You will be turned away without a reservation.

Reserve online at www.paralanaturaleza.org by going to the "menu", then "visit us" and then searching through the available tours for Hacienda Buena Vista. You can also call 787-722-5882.

Plan for a 90 minute walking tour; considered an "easy" walk by many.

Side note: The Para La Naturaleza website has various tours available for attractions all around the island so please read the description carefully before booking any tour to ensure you are booking the correct location.

Whereabouts: Barrio Magüeyes, Puerto Rico Hacienda Buena Vista, Ponce. About 2 hours from San Juan.

Address: Km 17.3, PR-123, Ponce, 00728, Puerto Rico

The Way: State Rd. 10 north of Ponce to to PR-123; Keep left to continue on PR-9, Sharp right onto PR-123 drive to KM 17.3 on PR-123

Activity Expense: $12 adults, $10 seniors and $9 children

Best time to visit: 10:00 a.m.

"THE TOMB OF THE INDIAN"

AKA La Tumba del Indio and Jayuya Cultural Center

Taíno History // Art

Whereabouts: Busto del Cacique Hayuya y Tumba del Indio; about 2 hours 15 minutes from San Juan
Address: Plaza Pública de Jayuya, 58-62 Cll Torrado, Jayuya, Puerto Rico, 00664

The Way: Take PR-140 to PR-141 to C. Mattei

Activity Expense: FREE

Best time to visit: open 24/7

Details: At La Tumba del Indio there is a monument of the Hayuya Taíno chief and memorial gravesite of a Taíno that can be viewed through a window any day or time. There is also a cultural center next to the memorial called Jayuya Cultural Center.

You can enter the monument and memorial area two ways. The main entrance is by stairs located on Calle Romero Barceló in front of the Nelson Rafael Collazo House of History Museum. The staircase is made with beautiful mosaic tiles with the Taíno names of Puerto Ricans towns.

The other entrance is located on Calle San Felipe in front of the Jayuya Cultural Center. Here you can learn about Juyuya town history, view photos and relics.

PUNTA TUNA BEACH AND WETLANDS NATURE RESERVE

AKA Reserva Natural Humedal Punta Tuna
& Punta Tuna Lighthouse
AKA Faro de Punta Tuna

Stunning Beauty // Beach // Trail Walking

Whereabouts: Southeast coast of Puerto Rico - Faro de Punta Tuna
Address: Cll. Catalina Morales, PR-760, Maunabo, PR, 00707

The Way: take Route 52 down to Ponce and then take Route 53 to Maunabo take Road 760
Activity Expense: Free

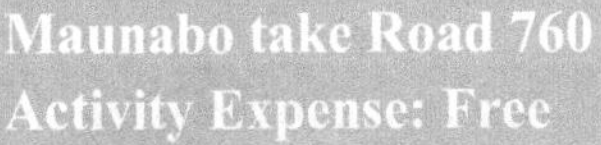

Details: This neoclassical styled lighthouse built in 1892 is quite a charmer with the cliffside ocean views that dreams are made of. It is still operational so visitors are not allowed inside but you can view the spectacular lighthouse and stunning beach below. Afterwards you can enjoy a day of relaxing beachside, trail walking, taking photos and birdwatching on the 110 acre nature reserve. Spend the day at one of Puerto Rico's most beautiful but lesser visited 1 mile beaches, Playa Larga AKA the Punta Tuna Beach. The Punta Tuna Beach is accessible from just outside the gate of the lighthouse. There is a fence lined trail that opens up to the beach. Unfortunately there are signs indicating strong rip tides at this beach so we do not recommend swimming. However, this is the ideal beach to have a more private experience to sunbathe, listen to some music, picnic and dip your toes in. There are some picnic tables available.

No lifeguards or restrooms, so bring everything you will need.
The reserve is also a Hawksbill and Leatherback sea turtle nesting site from March to July and home to 56 species of birds, so bring those binoculars.
The reserve has made efforts to be accessible to all with sand wheelchairs, audio tapes and tactile materials for the visually and hearing impaired. These items may be available at the visitors center, please ask.

The beach is the best place to take photos of the lighthouse.
The reserve's visitor center, Casa Verde is at KM 0.9 and the main entrance to the reserve is located at KM 0.5 on Road 760.
Call 787-861-0825, 787-861-0387 or email turismo@maunabopr.com for details.
Best time to visit: 9:00 a.m. to 4:00 p.m.

CAPILLA DEL SANTO CRISTO

History // Cliffs // Miracle

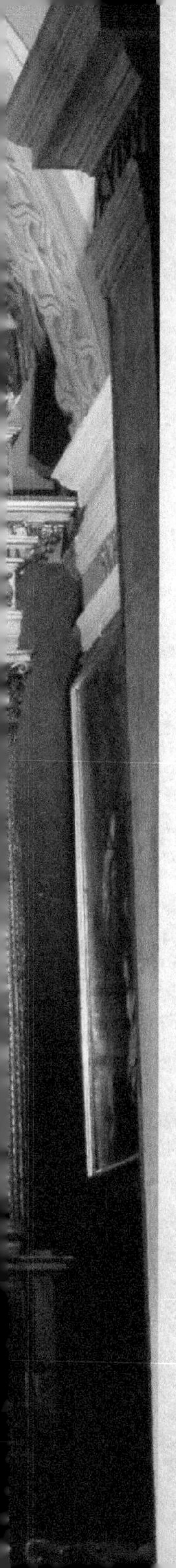

Details: Located in old San Juan on a cliff; this chapel of the Catholic Church is known for its healing powers. Folklore has it that in 1750 a horse and rider went over a cliff at the location during the San Juan Bautista celebrations. It is said that an onlooker yelled "Christ of Good Health, save him!" The horse did not survive but the rider did and construction on a chapel in that same location was started in 1753. Although it was later revealed that the rider actually passed away, people still flock to the chapel to pray for miracles.
Call 787-628-6099 for details.

Whereabouts: Capilla del Santo Cristo de la Salud, Cll. Del Cristo, Old San Juan, San Juan, PR, 009001
Address: 1 Calle Del Cristo, San Juan 00901 Puerto Rico

The Way: at the end of Cristo Street in Old San Juan

Activity Expense: FREE

Best time to visit: Tuesday, Saturday and Sunday noon to 6:00p.m.

THE PARQUE DE BOMBAS FIREHOUSE, THE HACIENDA BUENA VISTA MUSEUM

Historical // Iconic

PARQUE DE BOMBAS
1883

PONCE
ENGINE
CO
NO

Details: This former volunteer fire station originally built in 1882 is one of the most recognizable buildings in all of Puerto Rico. This firehouse closed its doors in the 1990's and is now a one of a kind small museum that offers an informative tour centered around the Ponce Firefighters. See photos, old fire trucks and equipment. There is a main level and also a photo gallery on the 2nd floor.

Call (787) 840-1045 or (787) 284-3338 for additional details.

Whereabouts: South central coast of the island in the town square Plaza de las Delicias in Ponce, P.R.
About 1.5 hours from San Juan
Address: Cll. Marina Delicias, Ponce, PR, 00731

The Way: Follow PR-52 to PR-1 W in Ponce. Take the Ponce Centro exit from Autop. Luis A. Ferré/PR-52, Follow PR-1 W, Blvr. Miguel A. Pou and C. Isabel-Muñoz Rivera to Cll Plaza Degetau/PR-1 in Segundo, Ponce, Puerto Rico

Activity Expense: FREE

Best time to visit: Wednesday to Monday 9:30 a.m. to 6:00 p.m.

PUNTA SANTIAGO NATURAL RESERVE

Aka Humacao Reserva Natural De Humacao Aka Reserva Natural De Humacao

Natural Beauty // Ghosts // Kayaks

Best time to visit: The reserve is open from 9 a.m. to 5:00 p.m. Kayak rentals Wednesday to Friday from 9 a.m. to 2 p.m. and Saturday and Sunday from 9:30 a.m. to 2:30 p.m.

Details: Bike, Kayak, paddleboat, Walk, bird watching. Water Sports and Ecotours is the company located in the Humacao Nature Reserve with the kayak and paddle boat rentals. This reserve is a special location known for environmental-conservation and its lovely coastal lagoons. You will experience a varied ecological community such as forest, coastline and halophytes (plants that grow in saltwater). This is a great stop for families and groups. For questions about kayak rentals, call 787-852-6058 and they have guided walking tours for groups of 10 or more available with at least 2 weeks advanced reservation. Email reservahumacao@gmail.com for additional details. Not in the mood for water activities? Take a tour of the reserve on bike - call 787- 559-7280 for bike rental information.

Whereabouts: Punta Santiago, Humacao, Puerto Rico, 00791, Puerto Rico, east side of the island
about 1 hour from San Juan

The Way: on PR-3 - Route 3 at about Km 75, just south of the Punto Santiago Beach on highway. Address: Park Entrance Rd.
Punta Santiago
Humacao, PR, 00791

Activity Expense: Entry to the Reserve and Parking is FREE. Kayaks and Paddle Boats are rented by a company called Water Sports and Eco Tours and the bike rentals are from Morillo Cycle.1 hour Self guided lagoon kayak tour is $15 per person. Paddle boats on the Mosto canal are $10 for 2 people; Bike rentals range from $7-15 per hour

WORLD WAR II MILITARY BUNKERS AT EL MORRILLO

There are many haunted areas in Puerto Rico but locals tell of ghosts in the abandoned World War II military bunkers at El Morrillo located next to the Humacao Nature Preserve. Don't worry if you do not happen to find any spirits lurking about as you will at least enjoy a one of a kind view of the Caribbean Sea and Vieques Island from this bunker.

El Morrillo bunker is about a 15 minute walk from the Reserve.

The way to the bunkers from Fajardo, road 3 south; from Guayama, road 3 east; from Caguas, road 30 southeast; located at km 74.3 of Rd #3, south of Punta Santiago beach. Walk or bike the main trail south (270m) until you see a trail crossing, continue southeast on Morillo trail (490m) until finding the beach, there you will hike a winding trail (200m) climbing southeast. Atop you will see two concrete (war bunkers) structures.

ARECIBO OBSERVATORY SCIENCE & VISITOR CENTER

Family Friendly // Educational // Interactive

Whereabouts: Northwestern side of the island - about 1.5 hours from San Juan
Address: Route 625 Bo. Puerto Rico, Arecibo 00612, Puerto Rico

The Way: Hwy 1 S/PR-1 S in Santurce from PR-26
4 min (2.6 km), Follow Autop. José de Diego/PR-22 W to Carr. Mariana Bracetti/PR-129 in Hato Abajo, Arecibo. Take the Highway 129 exit from Autop. José de Diego/PR-22 W
50 min (77.6 km). Follow PR-651, PR-635 and PR-625

Activity Expense: Adults: $15.00, Children $12.00 5-12 years old, Seniors 60+ with ID $12.00; purchase online in advance

Best time to visit: Wednesday to Sunday open from 9:00 a.m. - 3:30 p.m. - call to confirm days open as they may change seasonally.

Details: This is a recently renovated Science Center featuring a large exhibit area and auditorium. This interactive museum has an abundance to do and learn for all ages. It is famous for what you will see at the observation deck. There is a magnificent 1,000-foot reflector dish surrounded with incredible jungle views. Call or email to confirm as days of operation may change seasonally. They are also wheelchair accessible and have teaching materials in Braille. Contact information is 787-878-2612 Ext. 346 and info@naic.edu

Fun Fact: The Arecibo Observatory was the sender of the first message sent to space in 1974 and later in 2009. https://www.seti.org/seti-institute/project/details/arecibo-message

CAGUANA INDIGENOUS CEREMONIAL SITE

AKA Parque Ceremonial Indigena de Caguana

Details: Connect to a lost culture at this Taíno archeological site featuring sugar mill settlements, stone monoliths and petroglyphs. Once there you can download an app for detailed descriptions and explanations while on site for the perfect self-guided tour. Get an up close and personal look at the authentic exhibits on this property surrounded by beautiful mountains and a waterway.

If you would like the "complete" experience, call 787-894-7325 or 787-894-7310 in advance to schedule a guided tour. The tour guides are known to be very knowledgeable and passionate in regard to the significance of the area; plan for about 1-2 hours.

Whereabouts: Western side of the island - about 2 hours from San Juan in Utuado
Address: Carr.111 Km. 48.6, Bo Utuado, 00641, Puerto Rico

The Way: Get on Hwy 1 S/PR-1 S in Santurce from PR-26
4 min (2.6 km) Follow Autop. José de Diego/PR-22 W to Carretera 10/PR-10 in Arecibo. Take exit 75B from Autop. José de Diego/PR-22 W
49 min (75.1 km) Continue on Carretera 10/PR-10 to your destination in Utuado

Activity Expense: $3.00 per person includes access to the site, a modest museum and parking

Best time to visit: Wednesday - Sunday 8:30 a.m. to 4:30 p.m., but call ahead to make a reservation to confirm they will be open.

MUSEO DEL NINO

Children's Interactive Paradise

Whereabouts: Northeast part of the island about 30 minutes from San Juan Museo del Niño de Carolina, Address: Ave. Campo Rico, Intersección Fidalgo Diaz Ave., Carolina, PR, 00982

Best time to visit: Friday, Saturday and Sunday - 9:00 a.m. to 5:00 p.m. Closed for certain holidays.
Days and hours may change seasonally, so call 787-257-0261, 787-257-0261, 787-641-2000 or 787-641-0958 in advance to confirm details. The website address is www.museodelninocarolina.com.

Details: For a special day designed just for kiddos this museum has some truly unique exhibits. Explore a real American Airlines MD-82 jet, an erupting replica volcano or take a boat ride through mangroves.

Adults must have a child under 18 years old with you to visit and children must have an adult to visit. Plan for 2-4 hours to explore. Definitely geared for families with younger children. Although older kids (14 and up) may really enjoy the go karts and paddle boats. Go early so you can ensure the time to experience all the exhibits as they may close at varying times.

Bonus of a playground on site. The $5 go kart ticket gets you a 5 minute session. Before you plan to use the go karts, note that all drivers must be over 4'8" tall, passengers must be over 3" tall.

Activity Expense: Completely FREE for visitors over 75 years old; this includes museum admission, mini zoo, go karting and paddle boats. Please review the following for all other fees.

Parking is down the street within walking distance from the entrance and will cost $3 per car.

	Admission	Petting Zoo	Go Karts	Paddle Boats
Adults 15-59	$10.00	$2.00	$5.00	$2.00
Kids 1-14	$6.00	$1.00	$5.00	$2.00
Seniors 60-74	$5.00	$1.00	$5.00	$2.00

The Way: via Expreso Román Baldorioty de Castro/PR-26
Fastest route now due to traffic conditions, San Juan, Puerto Rico, Continue to Santurce
4 min (2.7 km) Follow Expreso Román Baldorioty de Castro/PR-26 to Av. Roberto Sánchez Vilella/PR-72 in Carolina. Take the exit toward Puerto Rico 72/Avenida Campo Rico from Expreso Román Baldorioty de Castro/PR-26
10 min (12.6 km) Merge onto Av. Roberto Sánchez Vilella/PR-72
Continue to follow Av. Roberto Sánchez Vilella.

CENTRO CEREMONIAL INDÍGENA DE TIBES

AKA Tibes Indian Ceremonial Center

History Buff // Exploration

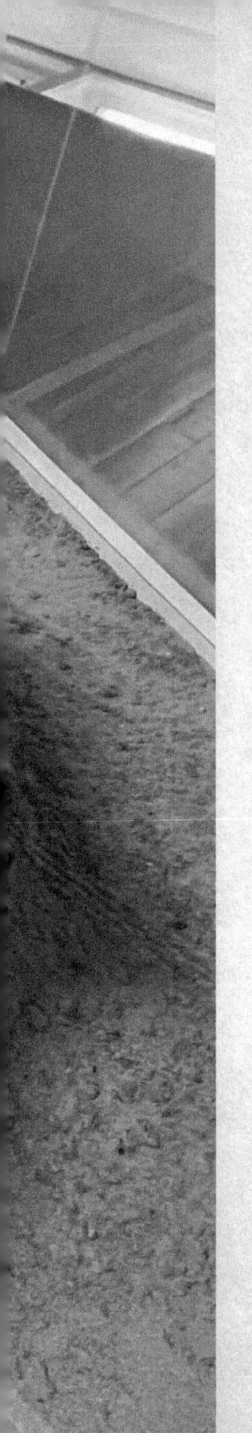

Details: Learn about *Taíno* history as well as the Igneri people of Puerto Rico. Artifacts have been discovered here dating back to AD 25, this is around the same time it is believed Jesus was crucified by the Romans. An easy flat walk around the grounds. If there are no guides available you can tour the grounds on your own. You will find ceremonial plazas and ball fields.

Plan for about 1 to 1.5 hours to explore.
Call 787-840-5685 or 787-284-4141 for details.

Whereabouts: Southern coast of the island - about 1.5 hours from San Juan in Ponce
Address: Carretera 503 k.m. 2.5, Ponce, PR, 00730

The Way: Route 10 north to Route 503. Turn left onto Route 503 and continue to KM 2.2.

Activity Expense: $3.00 for adults 18-75 and $2 for children over 5 includes access to the ground and museum. Adults over 75 and children under 5 are free.

Best time to visit: Everyday except closed Mondays from 9 a.m. to 3:30 p.m.but call ahead to confirm they will be open.

Awe-Inspiring Social Media Worthy Photo Gem Spots

BORINQUEN POINT LIGHTHOUSE RUINS

Aka Old Aguadilla Lighthouse Ruins AKA Las Ruinas AKA El Faro de la Ponderosa

Ruins // Photographers Love

Details: This is one of the original 15 lighthouses on the island and was built by the Spanish in 1889. It began operation on September 15, 1889. The former octagonal brick tower lighthouse is now in ruins with just a couple of sections of brick walls and stone. In 1918, a major earthquake severely damaged the lighthouse beyond repair. But locals and tourists still love to come here for the lovely views of the Atlantic Ocean and to take photos. Plan for about 15- 30 minutes.

Note: There are two lighthouses in Borinquen; the “new” lighthouse is on an active military base and is inaccessible to the public.

Whereabouts: Borinquen Ave (107) in Aguadilla Pueblo via the Borinquen Golf Club 18.4900, -67.1663

The Way: Go through the golf course. From Aguadilla, take Route 107 north. You will see large domes within the Rafael Hernandez International Airport. You will see a road on the left that will take you through the Borinquen Golf Club.
The road will become a dirt road and you will see the ruins. You can park very close to the ruins so it is not a long walk if mobility is an issue.

Activity Expense: FREE

Best time to visit: Before dark

YAUCROMATIC ART PROJECT

Urban Art // Family Photos

Details: Yaucromatic is a outdoor gallery project created by a non-profit. Featuring 62 works of art displayed throughout the town of Yauco. Murals and bold colorful walls with geometric shapes. Come here to take some awesome photos and have lunch at a local restaurant. Moderate difficulty of walking up hills and around the area. Please bring your walking shoes.
You can just park and start walking to see what you find or search the town facebook page for a map of the art to ensure you do not miss any. This is where you will find your official self guided tour plan.

Plan for at least 2-3 hours. It's suggested that you park near the plaza, where there is more space, and take your time while you walk around and enjoy the art.

Check out the project's official website at www.yaucromatic.com.

Whereabouts: Southwest side of the island; about 1 hour and 30 minutes from San Juan in the town of Yauco

The way: Driving from the San Juan area, you would take Route 18/52 south (through Ponce) to Route 2 west. From Route 2, you'd take Route 359 north to Route 127 west into the town of Yauco.

Activity Expense: FREE or you can book guided tours of the town via the Civitatis excursion website and searching "Guided tour of Yaucromatic".
Tours cost $15.00 per person and last about 2 hours.

Best time to visit: Daytime however busiest on weekends.

SANTURCE'S GRAFFITI SELF WALKING TOUR

Capital of Art // Photo Time // City Tour

Details: Want an extraordinary setting for selfies and unique family photos? Take a tour of Santurce's Street Art. Local artists put their heart and soul into these breathtaking murals with great cultural value. Visit during the day so that you can easily locate the art and murals. Plan to start your Santurce street art walking tour at the intersection of Manual Fernandez Juncos Avenue and Calle Cerra. At that intersection you'll immediately start seeing the street art. Continue walking north, up Calle Cerra where you'll pass by mural after mural. For several blocks you'll pass by vibrant expressions of art and soon see why Santurce is so special. Once you reach Calle Progreso, your walking tour is complete. Feel free to explore the blocks west of Calle Cerra as there is some street art that has trickled over to the surrounding blocks. Plan for a couple hours to get a good view of most of them.

Whereabouts: Northeast side of the Island about 10 minutes or 4 miles from old San Juan

The Way: via PR-26, Follow P.º Covadonga/PR-38 to Av. de la Constitución/PR-25/PR-26; Continue on PR-26. Take Av. Manuel Fernández Juncos/PR-35 to C. Cerra/PR-39 in Santurce, Turn right onto C. Cerra/PR-39

Activity Expense: FREE

Best time to visit: Daytime

ROADSIDE MONUMENT TO TRIBAL CHIEF MABODOMACA MONUMENTO AL CACIQUE MABODAMACA *AKA La Cara del Indio*

Photo Op // Taíno History

Details: This is a modern stone carving that honors the Taíno chief who fought bravely against the Spanish invasion of Puerto Rico. During the 16th century, Mabodamaca was the Taino Indian Chief of the territories that now are the cities of Isabela and Quebradillas. This sculpture was made by Isaac Laboy Moctezuma in 2002.
Although it's visible from the car, it's easy to miss. Visitors can park on the side road to take a picture and enjoy a local treat at the food kiosk next to the sculpture.
Plan for about 15 minutes.
As this is a roadside attraction located right on the entrance and exit to Av Noel Estrada - you will have to park across the street and cross a potentially busy road. It is located on the curved part of the road so drive slow when you are close so that you have time to pull over and park

Whereabouts: Northwest side of the island in Isabela, Puerto Rico
Address: Intersection of Rt. 2 & 113

The Way: about 1 hour 30 minutes from San Juan
Take the Hwy 1 ramp, Follow Autop. José de Diego/PR-22 W to Carr Puerto Rico 2 O/PR-2 W in Hatillo. Take exit 84B from Autop. José de Diego/PR-22 W, Continue onto Hwy 1 S/PR-1 S, Take the exit onto Carr Puerto Rico 2 O/Expreso John F. Kennedy/PR-2 W, Take the State Route 22 O exit toward Bayamón/Arecibo/Cataño, Merge onto Autop. José de Diego/PR-22 W, Take exit 84B on the left for PR-2 O toward Hatillo/Aguadilla/Mayagüez, Follow Carr Puerto Rico 2 O/PR-2 W to Av. Noel Estrada/PR-113 in Isabela Merge onto Carr Puerto Rico 2 O/PR-2 W, Turn right onto C. Marginal, Turn right onto Clljn Otero, Turn right onto Av. Noel Estrada/PR-113

Activity Expense: FREE

Best time to visit: anytime

Splurge Worthy Adventures and Activities

BAHIA BIOLUMINISCENTE DE PUERTO MOSQUITO

World Wonder // Relaxing // Once in a Lifetime

Details: Mosquito Bay is unfailingly the brightest bioluminescent bay on the planet. The bay will dazzlingly glow a greenish-blue hue when the water is disturb thanks to the Pyrodinium Bahamense. These single celled organisms can thrive in both fresh and saltwater. They live in enormous numbers creating a fascinating once in a lifetime experience. You will not be able to swim in the water as human interaction has proven to damage the Pyrodinium Bahamense.
Whereabouts:
Vieques Island off the East Coast of main island
The Way:
You would need to take a ferry from the main island and stay overnight in Vieques to see the best views of this magical bay. You can also fly there but we do not recommend it as this guide is all about maximizing savings.
The ferry ride is about 30 minutes from the main island. The ferry costs $2.00 for adults ages 13-59, $1.00 for children & adults 60-74 and free for babies 0-3 & adults over 75+
Tip: You might be able to bring your rental vehicle with you on the ferry but this is not recommended as the cargo ferries are known to be unreliable at times.
Activity Expense: The best way to experience this natural phenomena is by booking a kayak tour. A typical 2 hour tour costs roughly $50 per person. An awesome glass bottom kayak tour that we can recommend is by Bieque EcoTrips; www.biequecotrips.com but there are others to choose from.
If you are vacationing on the main island, we recommend planning for at least one or two nights of accommodation on Vieques Island as part of your trip. There are many heavenly things to see and do.

Best time to visit - for brightest of this phenomenon on display go on nights with very low moonlight or a new moon.

CASA BACARDÍ

Pina Colada // History

Details: Chances are you have tasted Bacardi or at least heard of this world famous Rum. Check out Casa Bacardi to learn the family history and all about the rum including the methods used to make it.
Try the Legacy Tour which is $30 (as of 2022) that includes a cocktail, guided tour and "Taste of the Casa"; which is a BACARDÍ Special Reserve rum which is not found anywhere else in the world.
If this specific tour is no longer available, check the website for tour options as the tour guides are known to be knowledgeable and interesting.
This is an english speaking tour and the tour/property is only for adults 18 or older with ID required.
For additional details contact 787-788-8400 or email casabacardi@bacardi.com.
Plan for 45 minutes to 2 hours depending on the tour and additional time to enjoy cocktails. Book tours in advance online. Great place for selfies and family photos as well with beautiful murals to be found on the property.

Whereabouts: About 20 minutes from San Juan, Northeast coast of the island
Address: Carretera 165 KM 6.2, Cataño, Puerto Rico

The Way: take connecting roads to Expressway 22 West toward Bayamon.Take Exit 7A, Road 165 toward Cataño,At the bottom of the exit, continue straight through the light on to Road 165.Take the third exit to the right. At the end of the exit ramp, turn right. Casa BACARDÍ main gate will be on the left.

Activity Expense: $30 to $75 depending on the tour

Best time to visit: tours are usually from 10 a.m. to 4:30 p.m., book online in advance

FLAMENCO BEACH AND "THE TANK"

Perfect Beach // History // Selfies

Whereabouts: A small island off of the east coast of Puerto Rico named Culebra. The beach and tank are located on the northern coast of Culebra.
Address: Flamenco beach, PR-251, Flamenco, Culebra, PR, 00775

The Way: Take the ferry out of the town of Ceiba close to Fajardo. The ferry takes about 45-90 minutes to reach Culebra. You must book your ferry tickets online months or weeks in advance as they often sell out.

Activity Expense: Beach $2.00 per adult and $5.00 per vehicle to park.

$2.25 for adults and $1.00 for children and seniors for ferry tickets. You can purchase www.puertoricoferry.com.

Transportation to beach from ferry terminal: Shared taxi or shuttle: $5 per person, private taxi to and from Flamenco Beach, $25 each way or rent a golf cart or car in advance for around $70 for the day. Beach chair rentals: $10 a day Umbrella Rentals: $20 a day.

Bring a rolling cooler with food and drinks with you to save money. If you can really splurge we recommend that you book overnight accommodation to more fully experience this little piece of paradise. So many wonderful beaches and restaurants to explore.

Best time to visit: take earliest morning ferry.

Details: Spend the day with sea turtles in clean calm waters with coral reefs that are perfect for swimming and snorkeling with all the amenities for a carefree day on this 1.5 mile long beach. There are also a couple of food vendors to purchase Puerto Rican foods from.The "Tank" attraction located at this beach is also an Awe-Inspiring Social Media Worthy Photo Gem Spot.This is where rusting graffiti-covered tanks litter the beach that was once used by the U.S. military for target practice. The seas are at times rough so not recommended for those with seasickness to take the ferry

ABOUT THE AUTHORS

Natasha & Natalia Martinez

Contact us at travel@natyheals.com with questions and comments and check out natyheals.com to learn about our other projects.

REFERENCES

Acevedo, N. (2021, July 1). *The world's oldest living man is Puerto Rican, Guinness World Records confirms*. NBC News. https://www.nbcnews.com/news/latino/world-s-oldest-living-man-puerto-rican-guinness-world-records-n1272921

Allen-Duenas, L. (2022, May 18). *Is Puerto Rico Safe? (INSIDER Tips for 2022)*. The Broke Backpacker. https://www.thebrokebackpacker.com/is-puerto-rico-safe/#:%7E:text=There's%20a%20high%20level%20of,d%20like%20it%20to%20be.

Amenities. (n.d.). El Conquistador Resort. Retrieved July 21, 2022, from https://www.conquistadorresort.com/amenities

Amigo Foods. (n.d.). *Top 11 Puerto Rican Street Foods & Drinks*. The Best Latin & Spanish Food Articles & Recipes - Amigofoods. https://blog.amigofoods.com/index.php/puerto-rican-foods/puerto-rican-street-foods-drinks/

Arecibo Observatory. (n.d.). *Welcome to The Arecibo Observatory | The Arecibo Observatory*. Naic.Edu. Retrieved July 24, 2022, from https://www.naic.edu/ao/

[Arroz con dulce]. (n.d.). Karma Free Cooking. https://karmafreecooking.files.wordpress.com/2009/12/arrozcondulce455.gif?w=455&h=455

Arroz con gandules. (n.d.). [Photogragh]. Wikimedia. https://upload.wikimedia.org/wikipedia/commons/1/13/Arroz_con_gandules.jpg

Bacardi. (2022a, April 25). *Visit Casa Bacardi Puerto Rico*. Bacardi US/EN. Retrieved July 24, 2022, from https://www.bacardi.com/us/en/casa-bacardi/

Bacardi. (2022b, July 1). *Buy tickets for Casa Bacardi Puerto Rico*. Bacardi US/EN. Retrieved July 21, 2022, from https://www.bacardi.com/us/en/casa-bacardi/tickets/

Barefoot travelers rooms & adventures. (n.d.). *Barefoot Travelers Rooms*. Barefoot Travelers Rooms. https://barefoottravelersrooms.com/

Benkhalti, S. (2021, June 25). *Empanadillas (fried Puerto Rican turnovers)*. Salima's Kitchen. https://salimaskitchen.com/empanadillas-fried-puerto-rican-turnovers/

Buen Provecho. (2019, May 28). Foodology. http://food-ology.blogspot.com/2010/02/buen-provecho.html

Cave of the Wind in Guajataca Forest. (2021, February 15). Puerto Rico Day Trips. https://www.puertoricodaytrips.com/guajataca-forest-cave/

Centro Ceremonial Indígena de Cagüana. (n.d.). Discover Puerto Rico. Retrieved July 24, 2022, from https://www.discoverpuertorico.com/profile/centro-ceremonial-indigena-de-caguana/7962

Coquito. (n.d.). [Photograph]. Wikimedia. https://upload.wikimedia.org/wikipedia/commons/e/e4/Coquito_in_a_glass.jpg

Discover Puerto Rico. (n.d.-a). *A Street Art Tour of Santurce*. Retrieved July 24, 2022, from https://www.discoverpuertorico.com/article/street-art-tour-santurce

Discover Puerto Rico. (n.d.-b). *Chorro de Doña Juana*. Retrieved July 24, 2022, from https://www.discoverpuertorico.com/profile/chorro-de-dona-juana/9210#profile-overview

Discover Puerto Rico. (n.d.-c). *Crash Boat Beach*. Retrieved July 24, 2022, from https://www.discoverpuertorico.com/profile/crash-boat-beach/8911

Discover Puerto Rico. (n.d.-d). *Visit the Coamo Hot Springs*. Retrieved July 21, 2022, from https://www.discoverpuertorico.com/article/visit-coamo-hot-springs

Discover Puerto Rico [dorimarrr]. (2021, February 22). *Facebook - Meld je aan of registreer je* [Facebook post]. Facebook. https://www.facebook.com/unsupportedbrowser?_rdr

G. (2022, January 18). *A Visit to the Tibes Indian Ceremonial Center*. Puertoricodaytrips.Com. Retrieved August 6, 2022, from https://www.puertoricodaytrips.com/tibes/

GFDL English Wikipedia. (2006, November 12). *Aguadilla Punta Borinquen Lighthouse Ruins* [Photograph]. Wikimedia Commons. https://upload.wikimedia.org/wikipedia/commons/a/a6/Aguadilla_Punta_Borinquen_Lighthouse_Ruins.jpg

Gonzalez, J. (2013, July 5). *View of Playa Sucia from Faro de Cabo Rojo in Puerto Rico* [Photograph]. Wikimedia Commons. https://commons.wikimedia.org/wiki/File:La_Playuela_(Playa_Sucia)_en_Cabo_Rojo,_Puerto_Rico.jpg

Government of Puerto Rico. (n.d.). *Travel Safe*. Travel Safe. https://www.travelsafe.pr.gov/

Heney, P. (2022, April 25). *Puerto Rico Travel: A Caribbean LGBTQ Haven*. TravelPulse. https://www.travelpulse.com/news/lgbtq/puerto-rico-travel-a-caribbean-lgbtq-haven.html

Jibarito. (n.d.). [Photograph]. Wikimedia. https://upload.wikimedia.org/wikipedia/commons/7/7b/Jibarito.jpg

La Playuela (Playa Sucia). (n.d.). Discover Puerto Rico. Retrieved August 6, 2022, from https://www.discoverpuertorico.com/profile/la-playuela-playa-sucia/8976#profile-overview

Lastras, J. (2009, October 11). *Ver artículo en mi Blog en* [Photograph]. Wikimedia Commons. https://upload.wikimedia.org/wikipedia/commons/d/d3/Morcilla_de_Burgos_%284006205518%29.jpg

Leafwell. (2022, May 23). *How to Get a Medical Marijuana Card in Puerto Rico in 2022*. https://leafwell.com/blog/puerto-rico-medical-canabis-card/

Light House Friends. (n.d.). *Punta Borinquen (Ruins) Lighthouse*. LighthouseFriends. Retrieved July 24, 2022, from https://www.lighthousefriends.com/light.asp?ID=1162

Mediavine Food. (2019, December 17). *Bacalaitos*. Latina Mom Meals. https://latinamommeals.com/bacalaitos-codfish-fritters/

Mofongo. (2006, December 17). [Photograph]. Wikimedia. https://upload.wikimedia.org/wikipedia/commons/4/41/Mofongo.jpg

Museo del Niño. (n.d.). *Museo del Niño de Carolina | Ciencia, Arte, Música y transportación*. Museo Del Niño de Carolina. Retrieved July 24, 2022, from https://www.museodelninocarolina.com/

Museo del Niño de Carolina. (2022, July 24). *Facebook - Meld je aan of registreer je* [Post]. Facebook. https://www.facebook.com/unsupportedbrowser

Norbert, N. (2022, May 16). *34 Fun and Interesting Facts About Puerto Rico You Probably Didn't Know*. GloboTreks. https://www.globotreks.com/destinations/puerto-rico/fun-interesting-facts-about-puerto-rico/

*PÃ¡gina Oficial Municipio AutÃ<sup>3*nomo de Cabo Rojo</i>. (n.d.). Http://Www.Caborojopr.Net/. Retrieved July 21, 2022, from https://www.caborojopr.net

Palacios, A. (2016, September). *Christopher Columbus and The Discovery of Puerto Rico*. StMU Research Scholars. https://stmuscholars.org/christopher-columbus-and-the-discovery-of-puerto-rico/

Para la Naturaleza. (n.d.). *Para la Naturaleza* |. www.paralanaturaleza.org. Retrieved July 21, 2022, from https://www.paralanaturaleza.org/

Parque de Bombas. (n.d.). Discover Puerto Rico. Retrieved July 24, 2022, from https://www.discoverpuertorico.com/profile/parque-de-bombas/8527

Pasteles De Masa (Puerto Rican Pasteles). (2021, December 31). Delish D'Lites. https://www.delishdlites.com/occasion/holiday-recipes/pasteles-de-masa-puerto-rican-pasteles/#:%7E:text=Made%20with%20a%20tropical%20root,Puerto%20Rican%20homes%20during%20Christmas.

Pernil Asado (Roast Pork Shoulder). (2021, January 5). Mexican Appetizers and More! https://mexicanappetizersandmore.com/pernil-asado-puertorriqueno/

POMARROSA COFFEE TOUR SCHEDULE. (n.d.). POMARROSA COFFEE. Retrieved July 21, 2022, from https://pomarrosacoffeelodge.com/coffee-tour/

Puente-Rolón, A. (n.d.). *Preliminary data on movements and macrohabitat use of the invasive snake (Boa constrictor) in Puerto Rico*. http://www.conservaciondeanfibios.org/uploads/2/1/6/1/21615192/18._preliminary_data_of_movement_and_microhabitat_use_of_the_invasive_snake,_boa_constrictor,_in_the_island_of_puerto_rico.pdf

Puerto Rico Day Trips. (n.d.). *Yaucromatic2: A Riot of Colors in Yauco*. PuertoRicoDaytrips.Com. Retrieved July 24, 2022, from https://www.puertoricodaytrips.com/yaucromatic/

Puerto Rico Travel Guide. (2022a, May 10). *Punta Tuna Beach & Nature Reserve Maunabo, Puerto Rico*. Retrieved July 21, 2022, from https://www.puertoricotravelguide.com/punta-tuna-beach-maunabo-puerto-rico/

Puerto Rico Travel Guide. (2022b, July 16). *Parque Nacional de las Cavernas del Río Camuy "Camuy River Cave Park" – Camuy, Puerto Rico 2022 – Updated Guide*. https://www.puertoricotravelguide.com/camuy-river-cave-park-camuy-puerto-rico/

Ramos, V. (2022a, July 7). *23 Puerto Rico Travel Tips from a Local (for 2022)* -. Travel Lemming. https://travellemming.com/puerto-rico-tips/#:%7E:text=Young%20international%20visitors%20thinking%20about,to%20be%2021%20to%20enter.

Ramos, V. (2022b, July 12). *42 Facts About Puerto Rico (Things to Know, By a Local)* -. Travel Lemming. https://travellemming.com/puerto-rico-facts/

Rivera, M. (n.d.). *Fast Facts About Puerto Rico*. Welcome to Puerto Rico. https://welcome.topuertorico.org/fastfacts.shtml

Rivera, M. (2022, January 24). *Pernil (Puerto Rican Roast Pork Shoulder)*. Sense & Edibility. https://senseandedibility.com/pernil-roast-pork-shoulder/

San Juan Puerto Rico.com. (n.d.). *Condado Beach - San Juan, Puerto Rico*. Retrieved August 6, 2022, from https://sanjuanpuertorico.com/condado-beach-hotels-resorts-san-juan-puerto-rico/

Santos, M. (2017, May 17). *10 Fascinating Things You Didn't Know About Puerto Rico*. Culture Trip. https://theculturetrip.com/caribbean/puerto-rico/articles/10-fascinating-things-you-didnt-know-about-puerto-rico/

Seven Seas Beach in Fajardo – Fun in the Sun! (2022, February 27). Puerto Rico Day Trips. https://www.puertoricodaytrips.com/seven-seas-beach-fajardo/

The Arecibo Observatory. (n.d.). *Overview | The Arecibo Observatory*. Www.Naic.Edu. http://www.naic.edu/ao/visitor-center/overview

The Sato Project. (n.d.). *Our Mission*. https://thesatoproject.org/our-mission-tsp

The William Miranda Marín Botanical and Cultural Garden. (n.d.). *Qué Hacer*. Jardin Botanico y Cultural de Caguas. Retrieved July 21, 2022, from https://www.jardinbotanicoycultural.org/recorrido-turistico

Trek to Gozalandia Waterfall in San Sebastian. (2022, March 25). Puerto Rico Day Trips. https://www.puertoricodaytrips.com/gozalandia-falls/

TripHobo. (n.d.). *Old Aguadilla Lighthouse Ruins, Aguadilla*. Retrieved July 24, 2022, from https://www.triphobo.com/places/aguadilla-puerto-rico/old-aguadilla-lighthouse-ruins

Uncover Travel. (n.d.). *Yokahú Observation Tower in El Yunque Rainforest, Puerto Rico*. Retrieved July 24, 2022, from https://uncover.travel/yokahu-observation-tower-in-el-yunque-rainforest-puerto-rico/

United States Coast Guard U.S. Department of Homeland Security. (n.d.). *170602-G-0Y189-510.JPG* [Photograph]. Https://Www.History.Uscg.Mil/Our-Collections/Photos/Igphoto/2002157861/. https://www.history.uscg.mil/Our-Collections/Photos/igphoto/2002157861/

USDA Forest Service. (n.d.). *El Yunque National Forest - Yokah Tower*. Www.Fs.Usda.Gov. Retrieved July 24, 2022, from https://www.fs.usda.gov/recarea/elyunque/recreation/recarea/?recid=43389

Walk on the Dry Side in Guanica. (2022, February 15). Puerto Rico Day Trips. https://www.puertoricodaytrips.com/guanica-dry-forest/

Walking, Biking & Kayaking in the Humacao Nature Reserve. (2021, January 3). Puertoricodaytrips.Com. Retrieved July 24, 2022, from https://www.puertoricodaytrips.com/humacao-nature-reserve/

Waymarking.com. (2011, January 23). *Monumento al Cacique Mabodamaca*. Retrieved July 24, 2022, from https://www.waymarking.com/error/error.aspx?aspxerrorpath=/waymarks/WMAKAZ_Monumento_al_Cacique_Mabodamaca

Wikimedia commons & yasmapaz & ace_heart. (2006, September 24). *Punta_Tuna_Lighthouse* [Photograph]. Wikimedia Commons. https://commons.wikimedia.org/wiki/File:Punta_Tuna_Lighthouse,_Maunabo,_Puerto_Rico.jpg

Wikimedia Commons, & Amarce, M. (2019, December 12). *Yaucromatic* [Photograph]. Wikimedia Commons. https://upload.wikimedia.org/wikipedia/commons/8/85/Yaucromatic.jpg

Wikimedia Commons, & Bermudez, J. (2006, July 5). *Caguana Ceremonial Ball Courts Site* [Photograph]. Wikimedia Commons.

https://upload.wikimedia.org/wikipedia/commons/8/84/Caguana_Ceremonial_Ball_Courts_Site_-_Utuado_Puerto_Rico.jpg

Wikimedia Commons, & Caraballo, J. (2018, July 15). *Cacique Mabodamaca* [Photograph]. Wikimedia Commons. https://upload.wikimedia.org/wikipedia/commons/9/92/Cacique_Mabodamaca.jpg

Wikimedia Commons, & Dwyer, J. (2007, December 13). *Tank_on_Flamenco_Beach* [Photograph]. Wikimedia Commons. https://upload.wikimedia.org/wikipedia/commons/9/94/Tank_on_Flamenco_Beach.jpg

Wikimedia Commons, & Miley, H. M. (2019, March 26). *Capilla del Santo Cristo de la Salud* [Photograph]. Wikipedia Commons. https://commons.wikimedia.org/wiki/File:Capilla_del_Santo_Cristo_de_la_Salud.jpg

Wikimedia Commons, & Nemčok, J. (2005, February 21). *Culebra pláž Flamenco* [Photograph]. Wikimedia Commons. https://upload.wikimedia.org/wikipedia/commons/8/80/Culebra_pl%C3%A1%C5%BE_Flamenco.jpg

Wikimedia Commons, & Rodriguez, R. (2014, October 19). *The Parque de Bombas* [Photograph]. Wikimedia Commons. https://upload.wikimedia.org/wikipedia/commons/7/74/Parque_de_Bombas_de_Ponce_Wiki-reduced.jpg

Wikimedia Commons, & Zulueta, J. (2014, August 17). *Street art in Santurce* [Photograph]. Wikimedia Commons. https://upload.wikimedia.org/wikipedia/commons/2/28/Street_art_in_Santurce%2C_Puerto_Rico.jpg

Wikipedia contributors. (2022, February 23). *Parque Nacional de las Cavernas del Río Camuy*. Wikipedia. Retrieved July 24, 2022, from https://en.wikipedia.org/wiki/Parque_Nacional_de_las_Cavernas_del_R%C3%ADo_Camuy

Yaucromatic — Arte Urbano en Yauco Puerto Rico. (n.d.). Www.Yaucromatic.Com/. Retrieved July 24, 2022, from http://www.yaucromatic.com/

Mondragon, M. (2022, April). Crash Boat Beach view.

Finca El Girasol. (n.d.). Discover Puerto Rico. https://www.discoverpuertorico.com/profile/finca-el-girasol/9189

Creative Commons Photo Credits:

Jose Kevo from Springfield, Missouri, EEUU (https://commons.wikimedia.org/wiki/File:Arroz_con_gandules.jpg), „Arroz con gandules“, https://creativecommons.org/licenses/by-sa/2.0/legalcode

charlene mcbride (https://commons.wikimedia.org/wiki/File:Coquito_in_a_glass.jpg), „Coquito in a glass“, https://creativecommons.org/licenses/by/2.0/legalcode

Minah / Flickr user: rosidae (https://www.flickr.com/photos/rosminah/) (https://commons.wikimedia.org/wiki/File:Jibarito.jpg), „Jibarito“, https://creativecommons.org/licenses/by/2.0/legalcode

Diane (https://commons.wikimedia.org/wiki/File:Mofongo.jpg), „Mofongo“, https://creativecommons.org/licenses/by/2.0/legalcode

yasmapaz & ace_heart (https://commons.wikimedia.org/wiki/File:Punta_Tuna_Lighthouse,_Maunabo,_Puerto_Rico.jpg), „Punta Tuna Lighthouse, Maunabo, Puerto Rico“, https://creativecommons.org/licenses/by-sa/2.0/legalcode

maryamarce (https://commons.wikimedia.org/wiki/File:Yaucromatic.jpg), https://creativecommons.org/licenses/by-sa/4.0/legalcode

Made in the USA
Monee, IL
24 January 2024

52268615R00077